The
Incredible
Human
Potential

This is the eye-opening story of the real gospel message of Jesus Christ—of how the missing dimension was withheld, and the whole world deceived.

BY HERBERT W. ARMSTRONG

It's positively astounding! It has remained undiscovered by science! No religion has revealed it! Higher education has never taught it! Is it possible the whole world has been deceived—regarding the awesome PURPOSE of human life—about the WAY to world peace and how it will come? And could it be true that the real gospel message Christ brought from heaven REVEALED this missing dimension—but was suppressed? This is the eye-opening story of the real gospel message of Jesus Christ—of how this missing dimension *was* withheld, and the whole world deceived.

Contents

Chapter 1

Christ's Gospel Was SUPPRESSED— Not Heard From the First Century Until NOW!

REPARE YOURSELF FOR THE MOST SHOCKING REVELATION OF YOUR life! Does it come as an astonishing shock to learn that the most important dimension in all knowledge was sent from God to this Earth by Jesus Christ—but that message was suppressed in the very first century? That Jesus Himself was put to death for revealing it? That His apostles, with one possible exception, were also martyred for proclaiming it?

Yet this message from the living God, if humanity had received and heeded it, would have saved this world from nearly all of its troubles, sufferings and evils.

The very word "gospel" means "good news." That message, when *fully* understood, reveals a human potential so stupendous—so awesome—it appears at first to be totally beyond belief, yet it has been suppressed from the world until now.

That message reveals the most necessary facts about humanity: what man *is*, the purpose for which mankind was put on Earth, where we are going, what is the way to world peace, happiness and universal prosperity, what are the true values, what is the awesome human potential, and how it may be achieved.

Answers to these questions form the most important knowledge ever made accessible to man. Yet it was spurned and rejected, and soon suppressed.

Christ's gospel message, when fully grasped, reveals what science has been utterly unable to discover. It reveals what religion in this world knows nothing of. It reveals what this world's higher education has never known or taught.

It reveals the most wonderful TRUTH a human mind could ever come to know! It reveals the missing dimension in knowledge, the knowledge most vitally *necessary* to know.

It was the most monumental good news ever revealed by our Maker to mankind! *Why* would men have wanted to reject it—hate it—put to death the Messenger who brought it?

Yes, *why?*

The answer is that *men* were DECEIVED! And all nations are deceived today!

The purpose of this book is to reveal HOW men were deceived and to make plain WHAT that good news really was. And *is.*

Nevertheless, it *was* suppressed. And that all-important revelation from the living God was not again proclaimed to the world until our present generation.

Even today, most of humanity has never heard the glorious *true* gospel. And those millions who do hear it have been so drugged and stupefied by false religions and counterfeit "gospels" that they only become confused. The TRUTH, indeed, is stranger than any fiction! Prepare yourself to read *astounding* truth—hard to believe, yet TRUE!

THE ARCH-DECEIVER

It is not intellectually fashionable today to believe in the actual existence of a devil, but biblical revelation says differently.

Biblical prophecies say plainly that in our time, today, the WHOLE WORLD would be deceived. Notice one such prophecy in the book of Revelation, chapter 12, verse 9: "And the great dragon was cast out, that old serpent, called the Devil, and Satan, *which deceiveth the whole world....*"

This Satan is revealed as the arch-deceiver who has deceived the whole world. But *how* did he manage to deceive the human race?

In the third chapter of Genesis he is shown as the deceiver of mother Eve. Through her, he caused the first man, Adam, to commit the first sin by a human.

When Jesus was born in Bethlehem, Satan was still here on Earth as the god of this world (2 Corinthians 4:4). He is also the "prince of the power of the air" today (Ephesians 2:2), holding sway over the whole of mankind.

Christ's message revealed the advance news of the total abolition of Satan's power over the world and his banishment from the Earth. It revealed that Christ was coming as his successor to take over the RULE of all nations. In Satan's mind, it was necessary for him to go all out to prevent that message from going to the world.

But *how* could he do it?

First, he moved to destroy the Christ child and thus prevent His growing up to proclaim that message. He influenced King Herod, the Roman provincial ruler over the land of Israel, and Herod caused all infants in Bethlehem and surrounding areas 2 years old or under to be put to death. But God warned Joseph and Mary about this, moving them to flee to Egypt with the infant Jesus until Herod was dead.

Again, when Jesus was about 30 years old, Satan sought to destroy Him spiritually before He qualified to preach a word of His message. But the supreme temptation with which Satan planned to ensnare Jesus became the very *test* which qualified Christ to depose Satan and to become ruler over all nations. Jesus thus qualified to restore the government of God on the Earth and to set up the Kingdom of God. However it was not in God's master plan for Christ to be inducted into that office until the end of mankind's first 6,000 years on Earth.

Nevertheless, Jesus proceeded with the mission for which He had come to Earth at that time. He proclaimed His message and taught it to His disciples.

Satan, however, still was the invisible power that swayed the world. Even though many of the Jews to whom Jesus preached *believed on* Him as the promised Messiah, they were swayed against believing His message—His gospel.

How did, and does, Satan deceive, move, and sway humanity? The amazing answer will be given later.

CHRIST'S GOSPEL REJECTED

Notice why and how the rejection of Christ's gospel happened.

In the eighth chapter of John, verses 30 through 46, you will read: "As he spake these words, many believed on him. Then said Jesus to *those Jews which believed on him*, If ye continue in *my word* [His message], then are ye my disciples indeed.... [B]ut ye seek to kill me, because *my word* [*His gospel message*] *hath no place in you.* ... But now ye seek to kill me, a man that hath told you the truth, which I have heard of God.... [F]or I proceeded forth and came from God; neither came I of myself, but *he sent me.* ... And because I tell you the truth, *ye believe me not.* ... And if I say the truth, *why do ye not* believe me?"

In due time, the Romans crucified Jesus. But He rose from the dead and ascended into heaven. From there, He sent God's Holy Spirit for His disciples.

Christ's apostles went out, as He commissioned them, to proclaim His message to the world. God's Church was raised up (A.D. 31) to back the proclaiming of the message. The Church began to grow, then "caught fire," and multiplied.

But Satan connived to set up a powerful Gentile religious leader with a counterfeit religion—the ancient Babylonian mystery religion. He hatched a counterfeit "gospel." He even appropriated the name of Christ, calling that religion "Christianity."

That, I know, is a breathtaking revelation, difficult today, 1,900 years later, to believe. But nonetheless, it is true!

THE COUNTERFEIT "GOSPEL" IS SET UP

In Samaria, north of Jerusalem, lived a Gentile people whom the Jews of Christ's day spurned, calling them "dogs." They had been moved there from areas of the Babylonian Empire about 700 B.C. by various kings, including Shalmaneser of Assyria (2 Kings 17:18, 21-24, etc.). They had brought with them into the land of Samaria their own Babylonian mystery religion. In the eighth chapter of Acts you'll read of their religious leader in the time of Christ, Simon Magus the Sorcerer.

Christ raised up the Church of God to stand back of the proclaiming of His gospel message by His apostles in A.D. 31. By A.D. 33, after a most amazing initial growth, a great persecution set in against God's Church (Acts 8:1). At that time, A.D. 33, this Simon the Sorcerer was himself baptized along with multitudes of others. He then tried to buy an apostleship in God's Church from the apostles Peter and John—but of course was refused and rebuked.

Thereupon this Simon appropriated the NAME of Christ, calling his Babylonian mystery religion "Christianity." Satan moved this man and used him as his instrument to persecute and all but destroy the true Church of God. Before the end of the first century—probably by A.D. 70—he managed to suppress the message Christ had brought from God.

There ensued "the lost century" in the history of the true Church of God. There was a well-organized conspiracy to blot out all record of Church history during that period. A hundred years later, history reveals a "Christianity" utterly unlike the Church Christ founded.

It had taken the NAME of Christ and applied it to the Babylonian mystery religion. It had replaced the MESSAGE Jesus brought from God with a "gospel" *about* the person of Christ—proclaiming the Messenger but suppressing the entire missing dimension from His message.

And for at least 18½ centuries the true gospel was not proclaimed to the world.

"ANOTHER GOSPEL" GAINS ACCEPTANCE

By about A.D. 58, when the Apostle Paul wrote his letter to the Galatians, many already were turning to this now new counterfeit "gospel."

Paul wrote: "I marvel that ye are so soon removed from him that called you into the grace of Christ *unto another gospel:* Which is not another [it was *not* good news]; but there be some that trouble you, *and would pervert the gospel of Christ*" (Galatians 1:6-7).

To the Thessalonians, about A.D. 54, Paul wrote, "For the *mystery of iniquity* doth already work …" (2 Thessalonians 2:7). It was the Babylonian mystery religion, started by Simon the

Sorcerer (Acts 8), a religion of iniquity—lawlessness—a religion rejecting the law of God. Much more of this later.

THE TRUE AND THE FALSE CHURCH

In the book of Revelation are pictured two churches, each of which go under the NAME of Christ. One, pictured in the 12th chapter, portrays the true Church of God, small in number, reduced through persecution and martyrdom, but obedient to God's law, and hated by Satan. The other, in the 17th chapter, called "Mystery, Babylon the Great, the Mother of Harlots and Abominations of the Earth" (verse 5). In other words, the Babylonian mystery religion steeped in "iniquity"—abolishing God's law.

During the time of Paul's ministry, these same Simon Magus ministers were troubling the Corinthians. Paul wrote to the Corinthians: "I am jealous over you with godly jealousy: for I have espoused you to one husband, that I may present you as a chaste virgin to Christ [the true Church, in the resurrection, is to be married to Christ, spiritually]. But I fear, lest by any means, as the serpent beguiled Eve through his subtilty, *so your minds should be corrupted* from the simplicity that is in Christ. For if he [a minister of Simon Magus] that cometh preacheth *another Jesus,* whom we have not preached, or if ye receive *another spirit* [of rebellion and disobedience], which ye have not received, or *another gospel...*" (2 Corinthians 11:2-4). (More, later, about the connection with the deception of the first woman, Eve.)

But notice, they were proclaiming *another Jesus*—as well as *another gospel*—and they followed *another spirit*—of rebellion and not obedience. That deception has continued through the centuries and is the state today. They took the NAME of Christ. They called their Babylonian religion "Christianity." But they not only presented a counterfeit *gospel* but a counterfeit spirit of *self*-centeredness and a counterfeit Jesus, completely different to the Jesus of the Bible.

Of these false ministers, Paul wrote further to the Corinthians: "For such are false apostles, deceitful workers, transforming themselves into the apostles of Christ. And no marvel; for *Satan himself* is transformed into an angel of light.

Therefore it is no great thing if *his ministers* also be transformed as the ministers of righteousness..." (verses 13-15).

PETER, JOHN AND JUDE EXPOSE FALSE MINISTERS

Peter wrote of these deceivers: "But there were false prophets also among the people, even as there shall be false teachers among you, who privily shall bring in damnable heresies.... And many shall follow their pernicious ways; *by reason of whom the way of truth shall be evil spoken of.* And through covetousness shall they with feigned words make merchandise of you..." (2 Peter 2:1-3).

John wrote of these same perverters of the true gospel, denying obedience to the way of God. "He that saith, I know him, and keepeth not his commandments, is a liar, and the truth is not in him" (1 John 2:4). "They went out from us, but they were not of us; for if they had been of us, they would no doubt have continued with us..." (verse 19).

Jude warned us that we should "earnestly contend for the faith which was once delivered unto the saints. For there are certain men crept in unawares, who were before of old ordained to this condemnation, ungodly men, turning the grace of our God into lasciviousness [license to disobey].... Likewise also these filthy dreamers defile the flesh, despise dominion [government], and speak evil of dignities.... Woe unto them! for they have gone in the way of Cain, and ran greedily after the error of Balaam for reward, and perished in the gainsaying of Core. These are spots in your feasts of charity... clouds they are without water, carried about of winds... twice dead, plucked up by the roots; Raging waves of the sea, foaming out their own shame; wandering stars, to whom is reserved the blackness of darkness for ever" (Jude 3-4, 8, 11-13).

THE WORD "GOSPEL" MISLEADING TODAY

Even the very word "gospel" is misleading today, especially as used by evangelical Protestants, their missionaries, their evangelists and their literature. The world has been, and is, full of "gospel programs" on television, on radio, in print, in personal evangelism.

Say to almost any person, "The gospel has not been proclaimed to the world for 18½ centuries," and he will think you are crazy, because it is the counterfeit "gospel" that has been vociferously proclaimed. But it is a "gospel" *about* the *person* of the Messenger, while IGNORING His message.

That gospel is based on the assumption that this is the time, and the ONLY time, when God is trying to "get the whole world saved." But those preaching such a message do not know even *what* salvation is, or how it is obtained.

How could the whole world be *deceived? What* did Christ's gospel MESSAGE contain that a powerful, invisible devil was so determined to suppress and to counterfeit?

Expect some sensational surprises!

Chapter 2
The Startling Revelation of What Was Christ's Gospel

W E HAVE SEEN HOW THE MOST IMPORTANT OF ALL KNOWL-
edge, sent by the Creator of all races, was suppressed
and another "gospel" foisted on a very deceived
and unknowing world. The world heard thereafter about the
Messenger, but not the message He brought. The time has come
when that awesome message must be revealed to the world.

WHAT, THEN, IS THE TRUE GOSPEL?

The true gospel is the good news that God sent from heaven
by Jesus Christ. That message, when *fully* understood,
reveals a human potential so stupendous it appears at first
to be totally beyond belief! It is *incredibly wonderful news*
revealed from the Creator.

It reveals the most wonderful TRUTH a human mind could
come to know.

It reveals what I term the MISSING DIMENSION IN KNOWL-
EDGE—the *most necessary* knowledge so vital to know!

That vital message reveals why humanity was put here on
Earth. That's vital knowledge science cannot discover, religion
has not revealed, education cannot teach.

Why? Were we put here for a PURPOSE? What is that
purpose?

Is there, after all, purpose and meaning to human life? A
purpose and meaning suppressed from human dissemination?

That's vital knowledge OUTSIDE the scope of today's science, religion, or education!

THE MISSING DIMENSION IN KNOWLEDGE

If there is purpose, what is it? Why were *you* born?

Where are we going? What is the ultimate transcendent potential of man? What is the way? *How* do we achieve that destiny?

What is *the way* to *peace*—among nations, between individuals, and between groups?

Why all this world's evils? Why can't we solve our human problems? There IS A WAY, and the true gospel reveals it! It's a basic law that *works* by inexorable and relentless force.

What is human nature? Did God create and instill it in humans to trouble us? Is it hereditary? How does it work? Neither modern science, religion, nor education can tell you.

What is the human mind, and *how* does it differ from the animal brain? Why, when the human mind can invent the computer and can learn to send men to the moon and back, can't such minds solve their own problems here on Earth and live at peace with their fellows?

What *is* man? Just what *are* we, after all? Science can't learn that secret, religions have never *rightly* explained it, but the true gospel, when *fully* understood, reveals the answer, and in truth!

What are the true values? What is important, and what is insignificant or of no value? Humanity dissipates its energy pursuing *false* values—spends its labor and its thinking in pursuits that are valueless and prove useless when achieved.

The true gospel, when *fully* understood, explains the origin of the devil. Did God create a devil to mislead and harass humanity? The gospel explains how Satan came to be the great—though invisible and hidden—POWER that sways invisibly and actually rules this world. It explains why Satan moved with all his wiles and subtleness to suppress, through humans he could sway, this vital gospel message which God sent by Jesus Christ to mankind.

Remember this: The true gospel message, had humanity *heeded* it, would have saved this world nearly all its anguish, troubles, suffering, and evils.

It is impossible for me, in a few words, to make it clear enough with sufficient emphasis to cause the reader *to comprehend* the supreme, tremendous meaning and importance of that *true* gospel message.

And even today, *when* heard, it is seldom *really* understood in all its colossal significance because Satan has thrown up such a smokescreen of false and counterfeit religions, "gospels," and teachings that the hearer or reader is left confused in doubt and unbelief—or in a state of indifference to the most important things in life.

Nevertheless, now just before the END of this age (Matthew 24:3), Almighty God has decreed that "*this* gospel of the kingdom shall be preached in all the world for a witness unto all nations..." (verse 14). This is the message the Eternal God is delivering now, by His end-time apostle, to the heads of governments in world capitals all over the world.

The true gospel, when viewed *with* all that it embodies— the reason for it, the prehistoric truth of Earth's first inhabitants, the reason humans were created and put on Earth, the CAUSE of all the Earth's evils and sufferings, the nature of the human mind, the need for spiritual salvation and what it is, the coming World Tomorrow of peace, what lies on beyond, and man's ultimate incredible potential—becomes the *most all-encompassing* subject that can enter the mind of man. Beside it, *everything else* shrinks to total unimportance. It is greater than any story of man ever written before.

WHAT WAS CHRIST'S GOSPEL?

God the Father had promised to send a messenger into the world from heaven, bearing a message from Him for all mankind. This promise is recorded in Malachi 3:1: "Behold, I will send my messenger, and he shall prepare the way before me [and *that* messenger, as explained in Mark 1:2, was John the Baptist]; and the Lord, whom ye seek, shall suddenly come to his temple, even the messenger of the covenant, whom ye delight in...." The "Lord," here, of course, refers to Jesus Christ.

That was the prophecy. The record of its happening is in the first chapter of Mark: "The beginning of the gospel of Jesus Christ, the Son of God" (verse 1). Then follows the account of

John the Baptist preparing the way before Him. Verses 12 and 13 record the temptation of Jesus by Satan, *wherein Satan sought to destroy Christ spiritually, before* He proclaimed a word of the message He brought from God the Father. More about this supreme temptation and test later. Then follow verses 14 and 15:

"Now after that John was put in prison, Jesus came into Galilee, preaching the gospel...." *What* gospel? "...the gospel of the kingdom of God...." That is the gospel Christ proclaimed. The message He brought was the message about the *Kingdom of God.*

That is the message God wanted proclaimed AS A WITNESS to all nations! But since the first century the world has known NOTHING of the Kingdom of God because that message was *not* proclaimed to the world after the first century.

That message, when explained and fully understood, covers a very wide range of revealed knowledge. It reveals—I repeat—what science has been utterly UNABLE to discover, what religion has never revealed, what this world's education has never known nor taught.

NOTE THESE POINTS

There are a number of points to be noted which are significant.

One is, that in Malachi's prophecy, Christ was called *a messenger bearing a message*—but moreover, He is called the *"messenger of the covenant,"* which carries very important meaning, to be explained later.

Again, notice the 15th verse of Mark 1. Jesus came into Galilee "preaching the gospel of the kingdom of God" and saying, "The time is fulfilled, and the kingdom of God is at hand: repent ye, and believe the gospel."

What did He mean, "The time is fulfilled"? And why was the Kingdom of God *then* "at hand," when it had not been *before* that precise time?

These points are of prime significance.

But first, before I explain more fully just *what* the Kingdom of God is, notice further that this definitely *is* the very gospel message Christ brought from God the Father—the same gospel the original apostles proclaimed—the same gospel the Apostle Paul proclaimed to the Gentiles.

CHRIST BROUGHT NO OTHER GOSPEL

Jesus said, "I must preach the kingdom of God to other cities also: *for therefore am I sent*" (Luke 4:43).

Jesus commissioned His disciples to teach the Kingdom of God. "Then he called his twelve disciples together, and ... he sent them to preach the kingdom of God ..." (Luke 9:1-2).

"But when they believed Philip preaching the things concerning *the kingdom of God*, and the name of Jesus Christ, they were baptized, both men and women" (Acts 8:12).

"And Jesus went about all Galilee, teaching in their synagogues, and preaching *the gospel of the kingdom* ..." (Matthew 4:23).

Jesus's parables concerned the Kingdom of God.

To His disciples, in explaining the parable of the sower, He said: "Unto you it is given to know the mystery of *the kingdom of God*," and then He explained to them the parable.

Again, "Then said he [Jesus], Unto what is *the kingdom of God* like? and whereunto shall I resemble it?" (Luke 13:18)—and then came a parable.

"And again he said, Whereunto shall I liken *the kingdom of God*? It is like leaven ..."—and then follows the parable of the leaven (verses 20-21).

One of His most important parables is recorded in the 19th chapter of Luke: "... he added and spake a parable, because he was nigh to Jerusalem, and *because they thought that the kingdom of God should immediately appear*" (Luke 19:11). Then He gave the parable of the nobleman going to a far country to receive for himself a kingdom and to return—the picture of Christ's ascension to heaven, where the coronation ceremony shall take place, and His return to Earth to rule all nations, as King of kings and Lord of lords, in all the supreme power and glory of the great God.

What gospel did the apostles and Paul proclaim?

DID APOSTLES AND PAUL PREACH A DIFFERENT GOSPEL?

After Christ's resurrection, the disciples were with Him 40 days. Were they talking among themselves about any *other* gospel during that time than the Kingdom of God? Notice, just before Jesus ascended into heaven. Luke had previously recorded what Jesus had done and said "[u]ntil the day in which he was taken up, after that he through the Holy [Spirit] had given commandments unto the apostles whom he had chosen: To whom also he showed himself alive after his passion by many infallible proofs, being seen of them forty days, and *speaking of the things pertaining to the kingdom of God*" (Acts 1:2-3).

Notice after His resurrection Christ was speaking to His disciples about "the things pertaining to the kingdom of God."

They, then, just before He ascended into heaven, asked Him: "Lord, wilt thou at this time *restore again the kingdom to Israel?*" (verse 6.) The apostles seemed never to understand that the Kingdom of God was not to be set up on Earth in their lifetime, even though Jesus's teaching—especially the parable of the pounds (Luke 19, quoted above)—should have made it clear to them.

After two years, from the inception of the Church of God on the day of Pentecost, A.D. 31, the counterfeit movement set in, headed by Simon the Sorcerer. The historic book of Acts records: "... And at that time there was a great persecution against the church which was at Jerusalem; and they were all scattered abroad throughout the regions of Judaea and Samaria, except the apostles.... Therefore they that were scattered abroad went every where *preaching the word.*" What word? Continue:

"Then Philip went down to the city of Samaria.... But when they believed Philip *preaching the things concerning the kingdom of God,* and the name of Jesus Christ, they were baptized..." (Acts 8:1-12).

The Apostle Paul spoke boldly at Ephesus for three months "disputing and persuading the things concerning *the kingdom of God*" (Acts 19:8). On a later trip, at Miletus, Paul called for the elders of the Church at Ephesus. Saying his farewell to them Paul said, "And now, behold, I know that ye all, among whom I have gone *preaching the kingdom of God,* shall see my face no more" (Acts 20:25).

At Rome, "there came many to him [Paul] into his lodging; to whom *he expounded and testified the kingdom of God...*" (Acts 28:23).

Again at Rome, "Paul dwelt two whole years in his own hired house, and received all that came in unto him, *Preaching the kingdom of God...*" (verses 30-31).

Did Paul preach any *other gospel?* To the Galatians he wrote, "But though we, or an angel from heaven, preach any other gospel unto you than that which we have preached unto you, let him be accursed. As we said before, so say I now again, If any man preach any other gospel unto you than that ye have received, let him be accursed" (Galatians 1:8-9).

But verses 6 and 7 showed that the Galatians had, already, turned to another gospel.

Jesus spoke of His message—the Kingdom of God—as the "word" that He spoke. The apostles, as you'll read all through the book of Acts, went everywhere preaching "the word"—meaning the Kingdom of God.

THE VAST COMPREHENSIVENESS OF A FULL UNDERSTANDING

I must call the reader's attention again at this point to the fact that a full and *complete* understanding of the message sent by God to all mankind, by His divine Messenger Jesus Christ, involves a vast comprehension of God's great purpose, and of events prehistoric, historic, present and future.

I might say it means an overall understanding of *everything!* Once understood, it will seem that the supposedly stupendous fund of knowledge disseminated in the great universities, is, in fact, infantile! It will seem as if man knows, now, almost nothing! For the missing dimension in knowledge is the all-important knowledge!

So I ask the reader to expect GREAT THINGS to be revealed in this and coming chapters.

THE "GOSPELS" BEING PREACHED TODAY

I have said that you hear many gospel programs today. One uses the slogan, "Preaching Christ to the Nations." One might ask, "Well, what's WRONG about preaching ABOUT Christ?" Or, "What's *wrong* about preaching a gospel of grace?" Or, "What's *wrong* about proclaiming a message about salvation?"

I have shown you the scriptures showing they started, even in the first century, preaching about a DIFFERENT Jesus—a Jesus supposed to have abolished His Father's commandments—who turned "grace" into license to disobey (2 Corinthians 11:4, 13-15 and Jude 4). They do not today preach the REAL Jesus, who said, "I have kept my Father's commandments," setting us an example that we should keep them also.

If those who claim to preach a gospel of SALVATION understood and proclaimed WHAT salvation really is—whether it is going to a PLACE, being changed into a different CONDITION, or WHAT—or WHERE—and HOW it may be obtained, it might be a part of the true gospel. But *today's "gospel" programs* do *not* teach what salvation *really is* or how one may receive it. When the blind lead the blind, they all fall into the ditch.

JUST WHAT IS THE KINGDOM OF GOD?

So it's time we come to UNDERSTAND just *what is* the Kingdom of God!

What is a kingdom? The Bible speaks of several kingdoms. The first world empire—the Chaldean Empire often called "Babylon"—was a kingdom. God inspired the Prophet Daniel to say to its king, Nebuchadnezzar, "…the God of heaven hath given thee a kingdom, power, and strength, and glory" (Daniel 2:37).

Then there was the kingdom of Israel—the family descended from Israel, which became one of Earth's nations or governments.

The kingdom of Israel was a forerunner of the Kingdom of God. It will be composed of the Spirit-born children of God—the Family of God, organized into a governing kingdom.

Therefore the Kingdom of God will be dual:

(1) A GOVERNMENT. A government—or kingdom—is composed of four things: (a) a KING, ruling over (b) people, subjects or citizens within (c) a definite jurisdiction of territory, with (d) laws and an organized system of administering them.

(2) A FAMILY (as the kingdom of Israel was a family of the children of Israel)—in this case the Family of God—a family into which humans may be born, which shall be a GOVERNING, or RULING, family that shall have jurisdiction over ALL NATIONS—that is, the WHOLE EARTH—and, later, the entire universe.

THE KINGDOM: A GOVERNMENT

Christ is to be the King of the Kingdom of God. He is the *Son* of God, whom He addressed as His Father. When the Church, by a resurrection or instantaneous *change* from mortal to immortal (from physical to spirit composition) becomes the Spirit-composed children of God, Christ will marry the Church, which shall become His wife. So we have Father, Son, wife, and children of the Father—all a FAMILY relationship— the divine God Family!

Notice, now, some of the prophecies:

"Therefore the Lord himself shall give you a sign; Behold, a virgin shall conceive, and bear a son, and shall call his name Immanuel [which means "God with us"]" (Isaiah 7:14).

"For unto us [Israel] a child is born, unto us a son is given: and *the government* shall be upon his shoulder: and his name shall be called Wonderful, Counsellor, The mighty God, The everlasting Father, The Prince of Peace. Of the increase of *his government* and peace there shall be no end, upon the throne of David, and upon his *kingdom,* to order it, and to establish it with judgment and with justice from henceforth even for ever. The zeal of the [Eternal] of hosts will perform this" (Isaiah 9:6-7).

The angel Gabriel is a super archangel—a cherub—one of only three mentioned in the Bible. It is recorded, "And in the sixth month [of the pregnancy of Elizabeth] the angel Gabriel was sent from God unto a city of Galilee, named Nazareth, To a virgin espoused [betrothed] to a man whose name was Joseph, of the house of David; and the virgin's name was Mary. And the angel came in unto her, and said, Hail, thou that art highly favoured, the Lord is with thee: blessed art thou among women. … And the angel said unto her, Fear not, Mary: for thou hast found favour with God. And, behold, thou shalt conceive in thy womb, and bring forth a son, and shalt call his name Jesus. He shall be great, and shall be called the Son of the Highest; and the Lord God shall give unto him *the throne* of his father David: And *he shall reign* over the house of Jacob for ever; and of his kingdom there shall be no end" (Luke 1:26-33).

When Jesus was on trial for His life before Pilate, the Roman ruler said unto Him, "Art thou a king then? Jesus answered, Thou sayest that I am a king. To this end was I born, and for this cause came I into the world, that I should bear witness unto the truth" (John 18:37).

However, Jesus also explained to Pilate that His Kingdom—His rulership—was not of this world—this time—this present age, saying, "*My kingdom is not of this world*... but now is *my kingdom* not from hence" (verse 36).

WHAT CHRIST'S GOSPEL WAS ALL ABOUT

I say Christ's gospel—the message He brought from God—was the advance good news of the establishment of the Kingdom of God.

But just what does that include?

And why is the Kingdom of God necessary?

Just how does it affect and relate directly to your personal and individual life?

Actually, Christ's message of God's coming Kingdom is directly concerned with world conditions as they are—with human nature—its source and origin—with world evils, suffering, unhappiness—with world peace. It's concerned with government—with the reason present human governments fail to be the benefactors of their peoples they are supposed to be.

His message hits directly at the very roots of individual personal happiness and at the awesome transcendent potential of each human life. It is concerned with the CAUSES of present conditions that affect every human and with the WAY that will solve all problems.

But it is concerned with far, far more.

It is concerned with God's tremendous, overwhelming, overall purpose as Creator of the entire universe. It's concerned with the entire vast universe, filled with its uncountable galaxies, nebulae, suns, stars, planets, and with God's purpose for them. It's concerned with all the angels—with the fact that one third of all God's created angels turned to SIN from which there can be no redemption, and God's great purpose and plan to prevent such a catastrophe happening to the other two thirds.

Most of these things are never remotely considered in religious teachings in this world. God's message is concerned with overall truth.

What has been covered so far should be considered as merely the introduction to the entire story of Christ's gospel message.

Chapter 3
The Incredible Human Potential at Last Revealed!

DOES IT MAKE SENSE TO YOU—WHEN HUMANITY HAS BEEN endowed with such tremendous mental power—that more than HALF of all people on Earth should be illiterate, living in abject poverty, near starvation, in filth and squalor; that in one country of 26 million people, only 3 percent can read and write and per capita income is only $69 per year?

Does it make sense to you that human civilization has developed modern science, higher education, the world's religions and its great governments, yet all these are in total ignorance of the *way* to world peace? None of these can tell us *what man is*, whether he was put on Earth for a purpose, what that PURPOSE IS, where *he is going* or *how to get there.*

Does it make sense to you—with man endowed with such great powers—that the world should be filled with so much unhappiness, troubles and evils?

Did God Almighty the Creator purpose and ordain all of this?

We may blame it all on human nature, but did God create man with this evil to harass him?

It's time to clear up this mystery. It's time we understand. It's time we come to the answer of these supposedly unanswerable questions that seem to baffle all human thought.

MAN HAS REJECTED THIS KNOWLEDGE

What is the most necessary of all knowledge to know?

It is the knowledge of what man is; the knowledge of why he is—the PURPOSE for which humanity was put on Earth; the knowledge of the way to achieve that purpose—of the way to world peace, peace between individuals, groups and nations; the knowledge of the cause of all the world's troubles and evils; the knowledge of the solution to all these problems; the knowledge of the true values—what is important and what is worthless.

That is the missing dimension in knowledge.

Look at the situation as it is now. Supposedly this is the day of enlightenment and mass production of knowledge. But both modern science and higher education have rejected the sole source of this basic knowledge—revelation—and no religion has given us this most-needed knowledge, though it is all contained in the book generally supposed to be the source of belief of at least three of the world's great religions.

Look at the situation as it was more than 1,900 years ago. Jesus Christ came from heaven with a message from God containing this knowledge. But even most of those who believed *on Him* disbelieved the message He brought and demanded His crucifixion for declaring it. His apostles went forth proclaiming the message; they too, with one possible exception, were martyred. Before the end of the first century, Christ's gospel *message* was suppressed and a spurious "gospel" proclaimed.

Go now all the way back to the beginning of humanity on the Earth. Our very first parents rejected this same revealed knowledge imparted to them by their Maker in person. They disbelieved *what He said.* Yet they did believe Satan's lies. They disobeyed by stealing the forbidden fruit. They *took to themselves* the knowledge of what is good and what is evil. All humanity has followed their example ever since.

The Eternal God nevertheless has made this vital revealed knowledge and truth available to any willing to BELIEVE *what He says*—in His inspired book, the Book of books—the Holy Bible. This book has actually become the world's best seller. But this precious book has been interpreted and misinterpreted, distorted, twisted, misrepresented, misunderstood, and maligned as no other book ever has.

Humans have written uncounted millions of books. People BELIEVE what these books say, though they may be partly, mostly, or totally in error and devoid of truth.

People take *these* books literally to mean *what they say.* Yet of the Bible they will say, "You surely don't take the Bible *literally,* do you?" They will not believe *this* book means what it says. It is the very Word of the living God, but they refuse to believe what God *says.*

And thus disbelieving humanity continues stumbling on its way, piling up the mountains of human woes, discontent, unhappiness, sorrow, pain, suffering and death.

Yet the Eternal God of truth and mercy makes available even today—in this end time of the present evil world—vital, exciting, new knowledge to those willing to believe *what He says* and to *obey it.*

More than 50 years ago ON PROOF, I came to BELIEVE and OBEY.

And in His Word the living God has opened my mind to the awesome human potential—to the *missing dimension in knowledge;* to the CAUSES of all humanity's evils and to the WAY to world peace and how it finally is *going to come.* And the same God of all creation is now opening before me the doors to unusual favor in the eyes of heads of state all over the world as an ambassador without human portfolio for world peace and a builder of bridges for peace between nations.

THE VAST UNIVERSE—AND MAN

In this Book of all books, God reveals Himself as Creator of all, not merely the Earth and man, but the *entire limitless universe.* The Maker of mankind is also the Creator of all. On a clear, cloudless night one may behold the star-studded sky. Is it possible there is an unrealized connection between the galaxies with their mighty suns, their planets—and man?

In this true story of the *incredible human potential,* I deem it well to look first to the Creator's overall purpose.

Prepare yourself for exciting new knowledge—the incredible awesome potential for which humanity was created and put here on Earth.

Winston Churchill said before the United States Congress that there is a purpose being worked out here below. Few indeed know what that purpose is; yet it is plainly revealed.

And it's the most exciting, most wonderful, hope-inspiring truth that could ever be revealed.

GOD—CREATOR OF THE UNIVERSE

Did you ever wonder about the countless millions of shining stars you have seen on an otherwise black, cloudless night? Sometimes they appear like a stupendous skyrocket which has just burst out into a glittering cluster.

Many of them are tremendous suns incredibly larger than our sun. Probably most of them are surrounded by planets, like our sun is surrounded by Earth, Mars, Jupiter, Saturn, and the other planets of our solar system.

Haven't you wondered about them? Are any of them inhabited? Did they evolve, as most scientists—astronomers, biologists, geologists—theorize? Or were they created by an all-intelligent, all-powerful Creator Being? Were they created and set in space FOR A PURPOSE? Do any of the planets contain any kind of life, or are all like our moon—dead, decayed, lifeless, wasted, empty, uninhabitable? And *if* they are in a dead state of decay and lifeless, WHY would an intelligent Creator have created them thus?

Or did He?

These are indeed intriguing questions. Scientists are extremely interested in knowing more about these uncountable gigantic bodies out there in space. Science does not know much about the origin of all these mighty bodies. There are many theories—many guesses—many hypotheses—as to how they were formed—but not based on actual revealed fact.

Science generally rejects REVELATION as a basic source of knowledge. Although astronomers for hundreds of years have been curious about the stars in the sky, many devoting their lifetimes to this study through constantly improved telescopes, they have known nothing about the purpose—or whether there *is* a purpose.

In Pasadena, California, a short distance from [the former] Ambassador College is the world-famous Jet Propulsion Laboratory, operated by California Institute of Technology, devoted primarily to U.S. government and space projects. There they design and produce unmanned spacecraft to be sent into outer space to photograph and send back pictures of other planets in our solar system. In December 1974 one came comparatively close (26,000 miles) to Jupiter. It sent back photographs that revealed additional knowledge about this largest of our planets. They did not give any proof of existing life or of conditions capable of sustaining life.

Then on February 9, 1975, astronomers at the University of Arizona claimed to have discovered through a telescope evidence of water on Jupiter. This I consider highly improbable.

Of course, the planet Mars has attracted the widest attention. Haven't you wondered if Mars is inhabited—what kind of life might exist there? This very question has supplied the theme for science-fiction movies and a television series viewed by millions.

But *does* human life or some other form—either much superior to man, or much inferior—exist on Mars or any other planet? Science does not have these answers. But the many photographs sent back to Earth from spacecraft on the surface of Mars, and hence being much *nearer* Venus, Jupiter and Saturn than our planet Earth, at least INDICATE a total absence of life on any of these planets—or conditions capable of sustaining life.

It had been planned to try to land the unmanned spacecraft Viking on Mars on the 200th anniversary of the United States as a nation. Actually, this spacecraft, in appearance something like a huge, ungainly Tinkertoy, had been created at the Jet Propulsion Laboratory, Pasadena, California. The Viking was equipped to send back photographs from the very surface of the planet Mars.

Actually it did land on July 20, 1976. The Jet Propulsion Laboratory (JPL), operated as a government project, but a division of the California Institute of Technology, is located a short distance from Ambassador Auditorium in Pasadena. The JPL scientists had arranged to transmit the very first photographs ever taken on the surface of Mars to the Ambassador Auditorium so that a public audience might view the transmission of these pioneer pictures.

Naturally this transmission of the first actual photographs from a planet farther than our moon was of very special interest to me—not only because of the importance of the first pictures, but also because the Ambassador Auditorium had been designed and built under my personal direction.

Several people had been sitting in the auditorium throughout the night. I personally, in communication with the jpl scientists, arrived at the auditorium about 4:50 a.m. The first pictures began coming in on the large motion picture screen at about 5:10 a.m.

The pictures showed clearly to us precisely what is revealed in the Word of God—Romans 8:19-23, Revised Standard Version. All is waste, deterioration, a condition of decay. There appeared no evidence of any sign of life of any sort, or of conditions that could sustain life.

All indications are that *only* our planet Earth is a life-supporting planet. Others appear to be like our moon—dead, decayed, wasted and empty. Our Earth is part of the solar system, which is part of a single galaxy called the Milky Way. There are many other galaxies on beyond ours. They extend in space distances so vast the human mind cannot conceive of them in terms of miles, meters, or any measure of distance except light years.

So even though science knows comparatively little about the limitless universe, revelation tells us something amazing beyond words about them.

The first verse in the revealed Word of God says: "In the beginning God created the heavens and earth." The word "heaven" in the King James should be translated "heavens," since the original Hebrew is in the plural.

The ancient King David of Israel wondered about the stars and was inspired to tell us God created them.

CREATED—BUT WHY?

David was inspired to write, "Oh Lord our Lord, how excellent is thy name in all the earth! who hast set thy glory above the heavens. ... When I consider thy heavens, the work of thy fingers, the moon and the stars, which thou hast ordained; What is man, that thou art mindful of him? ..." (Psalm 8:1, 3-4).

It may be that King David was not given the revelation of the real connection between man and the stars of outer space, for he continues: "For thou hast made him a little lower than the angels, and hast crowned him with glory and honour. Thou madest him to have dominion over the works of thy hands; thou hast put all things under his feet: All sheep and oxen, yea, and the beasts of the field; The fowl of the air, and the fish of the sea, and whatsoever passeth through the paths of the seas. O LORD our Lord, how excellent is thy name in all the earth!" (verses 5-9).

David here limits man's dominion to the present—that which God gave mankind in the creation of man—the solid Earth, the Earth's atmosphere, and the waters and sea (as in Genesis 1:26-28).

That is the dominion man has *now.*

In the New Testament, written much later, far more is revealed.

INCREDIBLE HUMAN POTENTIAL REVEALED

In the book of Hebrews we read: "For unto the angels hath he [God] not put in subjection the world to come, whereof we speak" (Hebrews 2:5). The theme of the context here is "the world to come."

There is but one Earth, but the Bible speaks of three worlds, ages, or civilizations on the Earth—the "world that then was" (the antediluvian world from Adam to Noah); this "present evil world" (from the Flood until Christ's return, yet future); and "the world to come" (which starts when Christ comes and sets up the Kingdom of God).

This verse speaks of angels as if the world had been put in subjection to angels; in fact, in the very beginning of this book of Hebrews, the first chapter, it is speaking of Christ and angels and the relation of angels to humans. This must be explained a little later.

But bear in mind the general theme here, or context, is "the world to come, whereof we speak"—not this present age, now coming rapidly to its *end!* Continue on in verse 6: "But one in a certain place testified, saying ...." Then follows a quotation from the first six verses *only* of the eighth Psalm.

In this Psalm, David continued showing specifically that God has now placed in subjection under man the solid Earth, the Earth's atmosphere or air, and the sea. But now the writer of the book of Hebrews is inspired to follow with something radically *different*—something to happen in the world to come!

This revealed knowledge of God's purpose for mankind—of man's incredible awesome potential—staggers the imagination. Science knows nothing of it—no religion reveals it, so far as I know—and certainly higher education is in utter ignorance of it.

Nevertheless, it is what God says He has prepared for them that love Him (1 Corinthians 2:9-10).

I have said before that God revealed necessary knowledge to our first parents, but *they didn't believe what He said!* Some 4,000 years later, Jesus Christ appeared on Earth with a message direct from God the Father in heaven, revealing the same necessary knowledge—but only a handful—120—believed what He said, though many professed to "believe on him" (as in John 8:30-31, 37-38, 40, 45-46).

Today science, religion and education still do not believe WHAT HE SAID.

I will explain this—and why—a bit later. But so many of these interrelated points cannot be explained all at once.

But now let's see what is said in this passage in Hebrews, beginning where Hebrews leaves off quoting the eighth Psalm: "Thou hast put all things in subjection under his [man's] feet. For in that he [God] put all in subjection under him [man], he [God] left NOTHING that is not put under him" (Hebrews 2:8).

Is it possible God could mean what He says ("all things")? *Nothing* excluded?

In the first chapter, the Moffatt translation of the Bible renders the Greek word translated "all things" as "the universe."

In other words, for those willing to believe what God says, He says that He has decreed the entire universe—with all its galaxies, its countless suns and planets—*everything*—will be put under man's subjection.

But *wait a moment!* Before you disbelieve, read the next words in the same eighth verse: "But now we see *not yet* all things [the endless universe] put under him [man]." Remember (verse 5), this is speaking of the "world to come"—not today's world. But what do we see now, today? "But we see Jesus, who was made a little lower than the angels [or, "for a little while lower"] for the suffering of death, crowned with glory and honour..." (verse 9). Man, other than Christ, is NOT YET "crowned with glory and honour."

But see how Christ is already crowned with glory and honor. Continue: "For it became him, for whom are *all things* [the entire universe], and by whom are all things, in bringing many sons unto glory, to make the captain of their salvation perfect through sufferings.... [F]or which cause he [Christ] is not ashamed to call them brethren" (verses 10-11).

In other words, Christians having God's Spirit are joint-heirs with Christ to INHERIT all that Christ already has inherited. He is now in glory! He has already inherited the entire universe. He *sustains* it by His power. Man, if he is converted, having God's Holy Spirit (Romans 8:9), is now only an HEIR— *not yet* a possessor.

But see now how Christ already *has been* crowned with glory and honor—and is already in possession—has already inherited. Begin with Hebrews, chapter 1: "God... [h]ath in these last days spoken unto us by his Son, whom he hath appointed heir of all things [the entire universe], by whom also he made the worlds; Who being the brightness of his glory, and the express image of his person, and upholding [sustaining] all things [the entire universe] by the word of his power..." (verses 1-3).

The living Christ already sustains the entire universe by His limitless divine power. The passage continues to show His superiority over the angels—He is the begotten and born Son of God—angels are merely individually created beings. Angels are now administering spirits (invisible to us), ministering to us—to us who are now in lower status than angels—but who are *heirs* of salvation, when we, like Christ, shall become *born* sons of God (verses 4-14).

OUTER SPACE—PLANETS NOW DEAD

Now put this together with what is revealed in the eighth chapter of Romans.

Here it speaks of Christ as God's Son: "... that he might be the *firstborn* among many brethren" (Romans 8:29). Humans having God's Holy Spirit are *heirs* of God and joint heirs with Christ—who, alone of all humans, has already been born as God's Son by a resurrection from the dead (Romans 1:4). He is the FIRST of the human family to be born into the Family of God—the Kingdom of God. He is our Pioneer who has gone on before. We shall follow at the resurrection of the just at Christ's return to Earth in supreme power and glory.

This eighth chapter of Romans, verse 9, says if we have within us the Holy Spirit of God we are His begotten sons, but if we do not have His Spirit we are none of His—not Christians at all. But verse 11 says that if we have God's Holy Spirit growing within and leading us we shall be raised from the dead by His Spirit—(or if living when Christ comes we shall be changed from mortal to immortal).

Now continue: "For as many as are led by the Spirit of God, they are the sons of God.... The Spirit itself beareth witness with our spirit, that we are the children of God: And if children, then heirs; heirs of God, and joint-heirs with Christ, if so be that we [in this life] suffer with him, that we may be also glorified together. For I reckon that the sufferings of this present time are not worthy to be compared with the glory which shall be revealed in us" (verses 14-18).

Continue, Revised Standard Version: "For the creation waits with eager longing for the revealing of the sons of God; for the creation [all the suns, planets, stars, moons] was subjected to futility, not of its own will but by the will of him who subjected it in hope; because the creation itself will be set free from its bondage to decay and obtain the glorious liberty of the children of God. We know that the whole creation [stars, suns, and moons now in decay and futility] has been groaning in travail together until now; and not only the creation, but we ourselves [we Spirit-begotten humans], who have the first fruits of the Spirit [the very FEW now being called to salvation—the "firstfruits"], groan inwardly as we wait for [the *birth*] as sons ..." (verses 19-23).

What an amazing marvelous revelation of knowledge!

No more amazing, awesome, eye-opening passage could be written!

It is so astonishingly revealing one doesn't fully grasp it just reading quickly through.

First I quoted from verse 29 of Romans 8 stating Christ WAS the firstborn of MANY BRETHREN.

In Hebrews 1, we see that Christ, the first human to be born by a resurrection from the dead, has been glorified and now sustains the entire universe. He is our Pioneer who has gone on ahead. At His return to Earth in power and glory those who have been converted and received God's Holy Spirit shall be born into the God Family by a resurrection. Then the *entire universe* will be put into subjection UNDER them!

Then, from Romans 8, *if* we have and are led by the Holy Spirit of God, we shall be raised to spirit composition and immortality in the God Family even as Christ was in A.D. 31 upon His resurrection.

Now once again from verse 19, "For the creation waits with eager longing for the revealing of the sons of God" (RSV). This shall happen at the time of the resurrection, when those who are human actually become—by a resurrection or instantaneous *change* from mortal flesh to spirit immortality—sons of God.

Now understand please. *Why* should the whole universe— the creation—be waiting with *eager longing* for the actual birth and appearing of all these sons of God, to be born into the Family of God? The following verses portray a universe filled with planets in decay and futility—yet as if subjected *now* to this dead state in hope! "[B]ecause the creation itself [the universe not now capable of sustaining life] will be set free from its bondage to decay and obtain the glorious liberty of the children of God" (verse 21, RSV).

How did all the planets fall into the bondage of decay? Surely God did not so create them!

Decay signifies a state or condition caused by degeneration and decomposition from a previous undecayed state. God, then, created these planets in a state of NONdecay. But something *caused* deterioration to set in.

What could have caused all this "bondage to decay"?

It cannot be the state in which God created them! Everything we read in God's revealed Word about God's creation shows it to have been a perfect creation. The Earth was first created a perfect creation of glorious beauty. Facts regarding that will appear in Chapter 4.

We shall see that angels inhabited the Earth prior to the creation of man. Angels, who were perfect from the creation until iniquity, or lawlessness, was found in them, caused the whole surface of the Earth to turn into a state of decay, confusion and emptiness, as we shall see.

Could the whole universe have been created capable of sustaining life? We are not told specifically by revelation in God's

Word whether it was or not, but what we are told throws additional light on why God decided to create man!

Continue this passage in Romans 8:22: "We know that the whole creation [universe] has been groaning in travail together until now" (RSV). Consider that the creation is compared to a mother about to be delivered of her child. The creation is pictured as groaning in travail in hope (verse 20), awaiting the birth by resurrection to immortality, of the children of God. It is as if the creation is the mother and God is the Father. Anyway, the whole thrust of the passage is that when we (converted humans) are born of God—then having the power and glory of God—we are going to do as God did when this Earth had been laid "waste and empty"—Hebrew *tohu* and *bohu* (Genesis 1:2). Christ, who renewed "the face of the earth" (Psalm 104:30), was renewing what had been destroyed by the rebellion of the sinning angels.

What these wonderful passages imply and indicate goes far beyond the amount specifically revealed.

To grasp the whole of the message of the Kingdom of God requires many chapters like this one. It is an all-encompassing subject.

This passage indicates precisely what all astronomers and scientific evidence indicate—the suns are as balls of fire, giving out light and heat; but the planets, except for this Earth, are in a state of death, decay and futility—but not forever—*waiting* until converted humans are BORN the children of God; born into the very divine Family of God, forming the Kingdom of God.

Jesus's gospel was the Kingdom of God. What I am showing you here is that Christ's gospel of the Kingdom actually includes all this knowledge here revealed—even the whole universe is to be ruled by us, who, with God the Father and Christ, become the Kingdom of God.

God is first of all Creator, but God is also Ruler. And He is Educator, who reveals knowledge beyond and outside the scope of human mind of itself to comprehend!

Put together all these scriptures I have used in this chapter, and you begin to grasp the incredible human potential. Our potential is to be born into the God Family, receiving total power! We are to be given jurisdiction over the entire universe!

What are we going to do then? These scriptures indicate we shall impart life to billions and billions of dead planets, as life has been imparted to this Earth. We shall create, as God directs and instructs. We shall rule through all eternity! Revelation 21 and 22 show there will then be no pain, no suffering, no evil, because we shall have learned to choose God's way of good. It will be an eternal life of accomplishment, constantly looking forward in super-joyous anticipation to new creative projects, and still looking back also on accomplishments with happiness and joy over what shall have been already accomplished.

We shall never grow tired and weary. Always alive—full of joyous energy, vitality, exuberant life and strength and power!

What a potential!

But *why!* Why has God purposed all of this?

There is still much to reveal. With this chapter, added to the previous ones, we have only started explaining the true gospel.

Why was it opposed? What is the cause of all human wretchedness and suffering?

What is the origin of evil?

What is the origin and source of human nature, and how shall humans be ridded of it?

Why was man made mortal, of material substance from the ground? Why does man, who is composed of matter the same as animals, who dies the same death as animals, have a mind thousands of times greater in mental output than animals, whose brains are virtually equal to human brain, both quantitatively and qualitatively? What makes the difference? *Why* is the human mind, while able to invent the computer and fly to the moon and back, helpless in the face of its own problems and relations with others here on Earth?

All these things will be explained.

Science has no answers; religion has failed to tell us; education is in IGNORANCE on these questions.

But read on, for the PLAIN TRUTH!

Chapter 4
Preexistence Before the Material Universe

I HAVE EXPLAINED TO YOU THE AWESOME POTENTIAL OF MAN. BUT *why?* Why does the Creator God purpose all this? Why did the living God decide to create man and put him on Earth? God does not do things without a reason.

To understand—to comprehend the whole picture in the order of time sequence—we must now go all the way back into prehistory. That missing dimension in knowledge, too, is revealed in the Word of God—God's message and revelation of knowledge to mankind.

Did you ever start viewing a motion picture when it was more than half way through? You probably were bewildered—not having seen what occurred before and led up to the point where you first began to see.

It's the same in coming to an UNDERSTANDING of what God has prepared for humanity—of the ultimate human potential.

True understanding can come only by beginning the story *at the beginning!*

If one should ask, where do you find the actual *beginning* of events in the Bible, most who possess even a slight knowledge of the world's "best seller" would say, "Why in Genesis chapter one, verse one, of course."

WRONG!

The real beginning, in order of time sequence, is found in the New Testament, in the first chapter of John, verse one. The events portrayed in Genesis occurred later—possibly even millions of years later.

But the event recorded in John 1:1 reveals an existence perhaps long prior to the time God created the Earth and the material universe.

Note it: "In the beginning was the Word, and the Word was with God, and the Word was God." It continues, "The same was in the beginning with God. All things were made by him; and without him was not any thing made that was made" (verses 2-3).

The term "all things" is translated in Hebrews 1:3, in the Moffatt translation, as "the UNIVERSE." The entire UNIVERSE was made by Him!

The 14th verse of John 1 says: "And the Word was made flesh, and dwelt among us, (and we beheld his glory, the glory as of the only begotten of the Father,) full of grace and truth."

The Personage called the Word was the one who ultimately—yet more than 1,900 years ago—was born Jesus Christ.

The name, "the Word," is translated from the original Greek text, and means, literally, just what is translated into English—"Spokesman." But He was not the Son of God "in the beginning." Yet the Scriptures reveal that He has always existed, and always will—"from eternity to eternity." He was "[w]ithout father, without mother, without descent, having neither beginning of days, nor end of life ..." (Hebrews 7:3).

So *think* on this, if you will!

Originally there existed *only* these two spirit Personages, self-existent. They had creative powers—they had perfect supreme minds—they possessed perfect, holy and righteous CHARACTER.

But THERE WAS NONE ELSE—NOTHING ELSE! There was no matter—no material universe—YET! No other living being or thing.

Only these two, equal in mind and powers, except that God was supreme in authority, and the Word in perfect harmony *under* that authority. They were of one mind, in absolute agreement.

But ALL THINGS—the universe and everything existing in it—were made by the Personage called the Word. Yet, as we read in Ephesians 3:9: "... God ... created ALL THINGS by Jesus

Christ." And prior to becoming Jesus Christ, He was "the Word"! Also, in His human life Jesus said He spoke only as the Father directed.

Yes, THINK!

In the eternity even prior to "prehistory" there were these two supreme Beings. Alone! In the emptiness of space! No other life forms—no other living beings! *Nothing else!*

But they possessed MINDS of supreme capacity. And, much, much later, they created humans after their own likeness and image. They endowed MAN with the power of MIND. It seems obvious that human minds were made to function in the same manner as the Creator's, although in an inferior way.

But how do we humans use our minds? We are endowed with something akin to creative powers. Man produces buildings out of existing materials. Man has produced intricate machines. But *how?* Man *thinks it out*—makes plans—before the actual making.

As an illustration: After much prayer about it to learn God's will, I was allowed to build the finest modern auditorium on this Earth—the Ambassador Auditorium in Pasadena, California. But I did much thinking and planning—I engaged the largest and best firm of architects and engineers in the world to design my general idea of such an edifice into finished PLANNING. We were 12 years thinking out, designing, and putting into actual plans and blueprints this auditorium before even breaking ground. Every cubic inch of the auditorium was designed on paper before a single cubic inch went into production.

How much more, then, must the great God and the Word have thought out, planned, and designed in their minds, before the actual creation?

They did not create matter first. The laws and facts of radioactivity tell us with certainty that there was a time when such matter did not exist.

But the great God through the Word first designed and created SPIRIT BEINGS—angels, each individually created—millions or perhaps even billions of them! They were composed wholly of spirit. They were given self-containing life—life inherent—immortality. But also God created within them MINDS—with power to think, to reason, to make choices and decisions!

THE SUPREME CREATIVE ACCOMPLISHMENT

But there was one super-important quality that even God's creative powers could not create instantly by fiat—the same perfect, holy, righteous CHARACTER inherent in both God and the Word!

This kind of character must be DEVELOPED, by the CHOICE and the INTENT of the one in whom it comes to exist.

So mark well this super-vital truism—that perfect, holy and righteous *character* is the supreme feat of accomplishment possible for Almighty God the Creator—it is also the means to His ultimate supreme PURPOSE! His final objective!

But HOW?

I repeat, such perfect character must be *developed*. It requires the free choice and decision of the separate entity in whom it is to be created. But, further, even then it must be instilled by and from the holy God who, only, has such righteous character to endow.

Perfect, holy and righteous character is the ability in such separate entity to come to discern the true and right way from the false, to make voluntarily a full and unconditional surrender to God and His perfect way—to yield to be *conquered* by God— to determine, even against temptation or self-desire, to *live* and to *do* the right. And even then such holy character is the gift of God. It comes by yielding to God to instill HIS LAW (God's right way of life) within the entity who so decides and wills.

Actually, this perfect character comes only from God, as instilled within the entity of His creation, upon voluntary acquiescence, even after severe trial and test.

I have devoted a few paragraphs to this point because it is the supreme pinnacle means in God's overall PURPOSE!

Now as to the prehistoric angels: God 1) created them with minds capable of thinking, reasoning, making choices and decisions with self-will, and, 2) revealed plainly to them HIS TRUE AND RIGHTEOUS WAY. But God of necessity allowed them free moral agency in accepting God's right way, or turning to contrary ways of their own devising.

What was God's ULTIMATE OBJECTIVE for the angels? Beyond question it is that which, now, because of angelic rebellion, has become the transcendent potential of humans!

As the testing ground, and opportunity for positive and active creative accomplishment, God created—brought into existence—the entire vast material universe.

God now created not only matter, but with and in it energy and such laws as man has discovered in the fields of physics and chemistry. God formed matter to be present in both the organic and the inorganic states.

And so we come now to that which is revealed in Genesis 1:1: "In the beginning [of the physical universe] God created the heavens and the earth."

As previously stated, in the King James English-language translation (AV) will be found the word "heaven" in the singular. But this originally was written by Moses in Hebrew. And in the Hebrew the word is in the plural—"heavens"—thus including not only our Earth, but the entire material UNIVERSE.

It is therefore indicated that *at that time*—after the creation of angels—the entire universe was brought into existence at the same time as the creation of our Earth. I find strong indication of this in other biblical internal evidence.

THE PERFECT CREATION

The original Hebrew words (the words originally written by Moses) imply a perfect creation. God reveals Himself as Creator of perfection, light and beauty. Every reference in the Bible describes the condition of any completed phase of God's creation as "very good"—perfect.

This first verse of the Bible actually speaks of the original PHYSICAL creation in its entirety—the universe—*including* the Earth, perhaps millions of years ago—as a perfect creation, beautiful and perfect as far as its creation was a finished, completed work. God is a perfectionist!

In Job 38:4, 7, God is speaking specifically of the creation of this Earth. He said all the angels (created "sons of God") shouted for joy at the creation of the Earth. This reveals that angels were created *before the creation of the Earth*—and probably before the *material* universe. The suns, planets and astral bodies are material substance. Angels are individually created spirit beings, composed solely of spirit.

It will come as a surprise to many to learn that angels

inhabited this Earth BEFORE the creation of man. This passage from Job implies it.

ANGELS ON EARTH SINNED

Other passages place angels on Earth prior to man.

Notice 2 Peter 2:4-6. First in time order were "angels that sinned." Next in time sequence, the antediluvian world beginning with Adam, carrying through to the Flood. After that, Sodom and Gomorrah.

This Book of books, containing the revealed knowledge of the Creator God, tells us that God created angels as composed of spirit. But can you imagine angels becoming *sinning* angels? Angels were created with power of thought, of decision and of choice, else they have no individuality or character. Since *sin* is the transgression of God's law, these angels rebelled against God's law, the basis of God's government.

Notice carefully what is revealed in 2 Peter 2:4-5: "For if God spared not the angels that sinned, but cast them down to hell, and delivered them into chains of darkness, to be reserved unto judgment; And spared not the old world, but saved Noah the eighth person, a preacher of righteousness, bringing in the flood upon the world of the ungodly."

These verses show that universal sin brings universal destruction to the physical Earth. The antediluvian sin, culminating with the Flood, was worldwide, universal sin. Notice: "... the earth *was filled* with violence.... [F]or *all flesh* had corrupted his way upon the earth ... for the *earth is filled* with violence ..." (Genesis 6:11-13). "But Noah found grace in the eyes of the [Eternal]. ... Noah was a just man and perfect in his generations, and Noah walked with God" (verses 8-9). All flesh had sinned—over the whole Earth. But *only Noah* "walked with God." So, the Flood destroyed *the whole Earth*—all but Noah and his family.

The homosexual and other sins of Sodom and Gomorrah spread over the territory of those two cities. And physical destruction came to their entire area. The sin of the angels was worldwide; the destruction of the physical Earth was worldwide.

The verses quoted above place the sinning of the angels *prior* to the antediluvian sins that started with Adam, *prior* to the creation of man. And *that* should be a surprise revealing of one phase of the missing dimension in knowledge! Angels inhabited this Earth *before* the creation of man.

And the government of God was administered on Earth until the rebellion of the sinning angels.

How long these angels inhabited the Earth before the creation of man is not revealed. It might have been millions—or even billions—of years. More on that later. But these angels sinned. Sin is the transgression of God's law (1 John 3:4). And God's law is the basis of God's government. So we know these angels, apparently a third of all the angels (Revelation 12:4), sinned—rebelled against the government of God. And sin carries penalties. The penalty for the sin of the angels is not *death*, as it is for man. Angels are immortal spirit beings and cannot die. These spirit beings had *been given dominion* over the PHYSICAL EARTH as a possession and an abode.

The universal, worldwide sin of the angels resulted in the physical destruction of the face of the Earth.

God is Creator. God is also ruler over His creation. He preserves what He creates by His government. What God creates, He has created for a purpose—to be used, preserved and maintained. And this use is regulated by God's government. When the angels rebelled against God's government, the preservation of the physical Earth and all its original beauty and glory ceased—and physical destruction to the surface of the Earth resulted!

God is Creator, Preserver and Ruler.

Satan is destroyer!

So, now, we read in Jude 6-7: "And the angels which kept not their first estate, but left their own habitation, he hath reserved in everlasting chains under darkness unto the judgment of the great day. Even as Sodom and Gomorrha, and the cities about them in like manner, giving themselves over to fornication, and going after strange flesh, are set forth for an example, suffering the vengeance of eternal fire."

Now back to Genesis 1:1-2. Verse 1, as stated above, implies a perfect creation. God is the author of life, of beauty, of perfection. Satan has brought only darkness, ugliness, imperfection, violence. Verse 1 shows the creation of a perfect Earth, glorious and beautiful. Verse 2 reveals the result of the sin of the angels.

"And the earth was [became] without form, and void...."
The words "without form and void" are translated from the
Hebrew *tohu* and *bohu*. A better translation is "waste and
empty" or "chaotic and in confusion." The word "was" is elsewhere in Genesis translated "became," as in Genesis 19:26. In
other words, the Earth, originally created perfect and beautiful, had now become chaotic, waste and empty, like our
moon, except its surface was covered with water.

David was inspired to reveal how God renewed the face of
the Earth: "Thou sendest forth thy spirit, they are created: and
thou renewest the face of the earth" (Psalm 104:30).

Now another surprise for most readers. Here is another bit
of the missing dimension in knowledge, actually revealed in
the Bible, but unrecognized by religion, by science, and by
higher education.

From verse 2 of Genesis 1 on, the remainder of this first
chapter of the Bible is *not* describing the original creation of
the Earth. But it *is* describing a renewing of the face of the
Earth, after it had become waste and empty as a result of the
sin of the angels.

What is described from verse 2 on, in the supposed "creation chapter" of the Bible, did occur, according to the Bible,
approximately 6,000 years ago. But that could have been millions or trillions of years after the actual creation of the Earth
described in verse 1!

I will comment later on the length of time it might have
taken before all Earth's angels turned to rebellion.

The Earth *had become* waste and empty. God did not create
it waste and empty, or in confusion. God is not the author of
confusion (1 Corinthians 14:33). This same Hebrew word—
tohu—meaning waste and empty, was inspired in Isaiah 45:18,
where it is translated "in vain." Using the original Hebrew
word, as originally inspired, it reads: "For thus saith the
[Eternal] that created the heavens; God himself that formed
the earth and made it; he hath established it, he created it not
in vain [tohu], he formed it to be inhabited...."

Continue now with the remainder of verse 2 (Genesis 1)
(the Earth had become chaotic, waste and empty): "[A]nd
darkness was upon the face of the deep [the ocean or fluid
surface of the Earth]. And the Spirit of God moved upon the

face of the waters. And God said, Let there be light: and there was light. And God saw the light, that it was good: and God divided the light from the darkness" (verses 2-4).

Satan is the author of darkness. The rebellion of the angels had caused the darkness. God is the author of light and truth. Light displays and enhances beauty, and also exposes evil. Darkness hides both.

The verses which follow in this first chapter of the Bible describe the renewing of the face of the Earth, yielding beautiful lawns, trees, shrubs, flowers, vegetation—then the creation of fish and fowl, animal life, and finally man.

THE GREAT LUCIFER

But first, before coming to man, we need to fill in the prehistory portion.

How did this sin of the angels come to take place? How did it start?

Remember, God the Creator *preserves*, improves and enhances what He creates by His government. What He creates is created to be used. This Earth was to be inhabited and used by angels, originally.

When God placed angels—apparently a third of all (Revelation 12:4)—on the newly created, perfect, beautiful and glorious Earth, He set over them, on a throne, to administer the government of God, an archangel—the great cherub Lucifer. There were only two other beings of this extremely high rank of cherub, Michael and Gabriel.

So far as is revealed, these are the supreme pinnacle of spirit-composed beings within God's power to create. This Lucifer was a superbeing of awesome, majestic beauty, dazzling brightness, supreme knowledge, wisdom and power—perfect as God created him! But God of necessity created in him the power of choice and decision, or he could not have been a being of individuality and character.

I want you to grasp fully the supreme magnificence of this towering pinnacle of God's created beings. Two different biblical passages tell us of his original created state.

First, notice what is revealed in Isaiah 14. (This famous chapter begins with the time, shortly ahead of us now, when the Eternal God shall have intervened in this world's affairs. The people of Israel—not necessarily or exclusively the Israelis or Judah—shall have been taken as captive slaves, and God shall intervene and bring them back to the original promised homeland.) "And it shall come to pass in the day that the LORD shall give thee rest from thy sorrow, and from thy fear, and from the hard bondage wherein thou wast made to serve, That thou shalt take up this proverb against the king of Babylon, and say, How hath the oppressor ceased! the golden city ceased! The LORD hath broken the staff of the wicked, and the sceptre of the rulers. He who smote the people in wrath... he that ruled the nations in anger, is persecuted, and none hindereth" (verses 3-6).

This is NOT speaking of the king of ancient Babylon, Nebuchadnezzar. The time is yet ahead of us—but shortly ahead. It is speaking of the modern successor of that ancient Nebuchadnezzar. It is speaking of the one who will be RULER of the soon-coming resurrected "Holy Roman Empire"—a sort of soon-coming "United States of Europe"—a union of 10 nations to rise up out of or following the Common Market of today. Britain will NOT be in that empire soon to come.

This united Europe will conquer Israel—*if* you know who Israel is today, and I do *not* mean Judah, known as the Israelis today. All that involves a number of other prophecies, which there is not room here to explain.

But this "king of Babylon" shall at the time of this prophecy have been utterly defeated by the intervention of the living Christ in His power and glory. Continue on:

"The whole earth is at rest, and is quiet: they break forth into singing. Yea, the fir trees rejoice... and the cedars of Lebanon, saying, Since thou art laid down, no feller is come up against us" (verses 7-8).

(I want to interpose an interesting bit of information right here. The cedars of Lebanon, biblically famous, are almost totally cut down. Only one small clump of these trees remains, high in the mountains. I have seen and photographed them. However, perhaps the finest specimen of the cedars of Lebanon surviving on Earth are on what was previously our Ambassador College campus in England. We prized them highly. It is interesting to see that this prophecy, written some

500 years B.C., should record the fact that these beautiful and stately trees should have been so largely felled.)

This passage in Isaiah 14 speaks of the doom of this coming king at the hands of the glorified, all-powerful Christ. It refers to him as Satan's chief political ruler and military destroyer, totally deceived by Satan in the years very shortly ahead of us.

Then, coming to verse 12, this human earthly type of Satan the devil suddenly transposes to Satan himself—the former archangel, Lucifer:

"How art thou fallen from heaven, O Lucifer, son of the morning! how art thou cut down to the ground, which didst weaken the nations!" A better translation here is: "How art thou, who didst weaken the nations, cut down to the ground." The RSV translates it: "How you are cut down to the ground, you who laid the nations low!" This the former Lucifer did through the human political-military leader in his power—spoken of in the first 11 verses.

The name "Lucifer" means "shining star of the dawn," or "bringer of light," as God first created him. Now continue: "For thou hast said in thine heart, I will ascend into heaven, I will exalt my throne above the stars [angels] of God..." (verse 13).

Notice, Lucifer had a throne; he was a ruler. His throne was on Earth, for he was going to ascend into heaven. Continue: "...I will sit also upon the mount of the congregation, in the sides of the north: I will ascend above the heights of the clouds; I will be like the most High" (verses 13-14). Actually, it is plain that Lucifer had nothing less in mind than knocking the Creator God off His throne and becoming supreme God himself.

Apparently he planned to put himself in place of God, over the universe!

But finally, as the context returns again to the human type: "Yet thou shalt be brought down to hell [Heb. *sheol*], to the sides of the pit" (verse 15).

From that point, the thought returns to the human king. Lucifer was the supreme masterpiece of God's creative power, as an individually created being, threatening, as a Frankenstein monster, to destroy his own Maker—and assume all His powers to rule the whole universe.

His rebel rule was NOT a government based upon the principle of love—of giving, of outgoing concern for the good of others, but based on SELF-CENTEREDNESS, on vanity, lust and greed, on envy, jealousy, the spirit of competition, hatred, violence and destruction, on darkness and error, instead of light and truth, on ugliness instead of beauty.

Look now at the other biblical passage describing this supreme angelic creation of God, in Ezekiel 28.

LUCIFER A CREATED BEING

Actually, the entire concept in chapter 26 speaks of the ancient great commercial city of Tyre. It was the commercial metropolis of the ancient world, even as Babylon was the political capital. Tyre was the New York, the London, the Tokyo, or the Paris of the ancient world. The ancient Tyre, port of the world's shippers and merchants, gloried *herself* in her beauty, even as Paris in our time.

Chapter 27 carries on with comparisons to passages in the 18th chapter of the book of Revelation referring to a politico-religious leader to come (verses 9-19).

But coming to chapter 28, the theme comes more completely to the time just now ahead of us, the same time depicted in Isaiah 14. Ezekiel 28 speaks of the prince of Tyre, an earthly ruler. God says to the Prophet Ezekiel: "Son of man, say unto the prince of Tyrus [actually referring to a powerful religious leader to arise SOON, in our time], Thus saith the [Eternal] God; Because thine heart is lifted up, and thou hast said, I am a god, I sit in the seat of God, in the midst of the seas; yet thou art a man, and not God, though thou set thine heart as the heart of God: Behold, thou art wiser than Daniel; there is no secret that they can hide from thee: With thy wisdom and with thine understanding thou hast gotten thee riches, and hast gotten gold and silver into thy treasures [or "treasuries"—RSV] ... and thine heart is lifted up because of thy riches: Therefore thus saith the [Eternal] God; Because thou hast set thine heart as the heart of God; Behold, therefore I will bring strangers upon thee, the terrible of the nations ‥‥ They shall bring thee down to the pit, and thou shalt die the deaths of them that are slain in the midst of the seas" (Ezekiel 28:2-8). (Compare with 2 Thessalonians 2:4, speaking of "that man of sin," "[w]ho opposeth and exalteth himself above all that is called God ... so that he *as* God sitteth in the temple of God, showing himself that he is God.")

WHAT A SUPER BEING!

But at this point, as in Isaiah 14, the lesser human type lifts to a greater spirit antitype. Instead of the prince of Tyre—a human man—it now speaks of the KING of Tyre. This is the same Lucifer.

Ezekiel the prophet continues: "Moreover the word of the LORD came unto me, saying, Son of man, take up a lamentation upon the KING of Tyrus, and say unto him, Thus saith the [Eternal] GOD; Thou sealest up the sum, full of wisdom, and perfect in beauty" (Ezekiel 28:11-12).

Please read that again! God would never say anything like that of a human man. This superb spirit being filled up the sum total of wisdom, perfection and beauty. He was the supreme pinnacle, the masterpiece, of God's creation, as an individually created being, the greatest one in the almighty power of God to create! The tragic thing is that he rebelled against his Maker!

"Thou hast been in Eden the garden of God ..." (verse 13). He had inhabited this Earth. His throne was here. "Every precious stone was thy covering ... the workmanship of thy tabrets and of thy pipes was prepared in thee in the day that thou wast created" (verse 13). He was a *created being*—not born human. He was a spirit being—*not* human flesh. Great genius and skill in music was created in him. Now that he has become perverted in all thinking, acting and being, he is the real author of modern perverted music—of discordant moans, squawks, shrieks, wails—unhappy, discouraged moods. Think of all the supreme talent, ability and potential in a being created with such capacities. And all perverted! All gone sour—all dissipated, turned to hatred, destruction, hopelessness!

Yet, take courage. The awesome human potential, if we care enough about it to *resist* Satan's wiles and evils and discouragements and to persevere in *God's way,* is infinitely superior and higher than Lucifer's—even as created, *before* he turned to rebellion and iniquity!

But continuing the particular revelation of this crucially important missing dimension in knowledge: "Thou art the anointed cherub that covereth; and I have set thee so," says God of this Lucifer (verse 14). This takes us back to the 25th chapter of Exodus, where God gave Moses the pattern for the ark of the covenant. The description begins with verse 10, and verses 18-20 show, in the material pattern, the two cherubs who were stationed at each end of the very throne of God in heaven—the throne of the government of God over the entire universe. The wings of the two cherubim covered the throne of God.

TRAINED AT UNIVERSE HEADQUARTERS

This Lucifer, then, had been stationed at the very throne of God. He was trained and experienced in the administration of the government of God. God chose such a being, well-experienced and trained, to be the king ruling the government of God over the angels who inhabited the whole Earth.

Continue: "…thou wast upon the holy mountain of God; thou hast walked up and down in the midst of the stones of fire" (Ezekiel 28:14). This is not talking about any human being. But continue: "Thou wast perfect in thy *ways* from the day that thou wast created, till iniquity [lawlessness] was found in thee" (verse 15). He had complete knowledge, understanding and wisdom. But he also was given full powers of reasoning, thinking, making decisions, making his choice. And, with all this foreknowledge—even of results and consequences—this superb being, the highest that even God could create by fiat, turned to rebellion against his Maker—against the way that produces every good. He turned to lawlessness. He had been trained in the administration of perfect law and order. As long as Lucifer continued in this perfect way, there was happiness and joy unspeakable over the whole Earth. There was glorious peace—beautiful harmony, perfect love, cooperation. The government of God produced a wonderfully happy state—as long as Lucifer was loyal in the conduct of God's government.

WHAT CAUSED THE ANGELS' SIN?

What caused the angels on Earth to sin, to turn to lawlessness? Certainly the ordinary angels did not persuade this great superbeing to turn traitor. No, it was in him that iniquity was found. But, after how long? We don't know. God does not reveal that! It could have been any number of years from one or less to millions times millions.

And then, even after Lucifer himself made the decision to rebel and try to invade God's heaven to take over the universe, it is not revealed how long it took him to persuade all of the angels under him to turn traitor and follow him.

I know well the method he used. He uses the same method still today in leading deceived humans into disloyalty, rebellion, and self-centered opposition against God's government. First, he turns one or two to envy, jealousy, and resentment over an imagined injustice—then into disloyalty. Then he uses that one or two, like a rotten apple in a crate, to stir up resentment, feelings of self-pity, disloyalty and rebellion in others next to them. And, as each rotten apple rots those next to it until the whole crate is rotten, so Satan proceeds.

If, in the government of God on Earth today, the "rotten apples" are not thrown out early enough, they would destroy the whole government. But, once thrown out of the crate, they cannot do any more damage to those in the crate.

But *think* how long it must have taken the soured and embittered Lucifer to turn millions of holy angels into resentment, bitterness, disloyalty, and finally open and vicious rebellion. It could have taken hundreds, thousands, or millions of years. This was all before the first human was created.

All this happened after the original creation of the Earth, described in verse 1 of Genesis 1. Verse 2 of this "creation" chapter describes a condition *resulting* from this sin of the angels. The events described in verse 2, therefore, may have occurred millions of years *after* the original creation of the Earth.

The Earth, therefore, may have been created millions of years ago. But continue this passage in Ezekiel 28: "By the multitude of thy merchandise they have filled the midst of thee with violence, and thou hast sinned: therefore I will cast thee as profane out of the mountain of God: and I will destroy [remove] thee, O covering cherub, from the midst of the stones of fire. Thine heart was lifted up because of thy beauty, thou hast corrupted thy wisdom by reason of thy brightness: I will

cast thee to the ground ..." (verses 16-17). At this point the context returns to the soon-to-appear, human, religious-political
ruler—of whom the prince of ancient Tyre was a forerunner.

Earlier in this chapter, I showed you how physical destruction, ugliness and darkness had covered the *face* of the Earth,
as the result of the sin of Lucifer (who is now the devil) and
these "angels that sinned" (now demons), and how in six days
God had renewed the face of the Earth (Genesis 1:2-25).

But why did God create man on the Earth? (verse 26).

Look at this situation as God does. God has given us
humans minds, like the mind of God, only inferior and limited. God made us in His image, after His likeness (form
and shape), only composed of matter instead of spirit. But
God says, "Let this mind be in you, which was also in Christ
Jesus" (Philippians 2:5). We can, to some degree, think even
as God thinks. How must God have looked at the situation, as
He started renewing the face of the Earth—after the colossal
debacle of the angels!

He had created a beautiful, perfect creation in the Earth.
He populated it with holy angels—probably millions of them.
He put over them, as king, on an earthly throne, the archangel—the cherub Lucifer. Lucifer was the supreme masterpiece of God's creative power as a single separately created
spirit being. He was the most perfect in beauty, power, mind,
knowledge, intellect, wisdom, within the almighty power of
God to create. God can create nothing higher or more perfect,
by instantaneous fiat.

Yet this great being, knowledgeable, trained and experienced at God's own throne in heaven over the universe and the
administration of the government of God, had rejected that
government, corrupted his way, rebelled against administering
or even obeying it. He had led all his angels astray and into the
sin of rebellion and disloyalty.

Now consider further. Apparently the entire universe had
been created also at the time of the Earth's creation. There is
no evidence either in God's revealed Word, nor in science, that
any of the planets in endless outer space had been inhabited
with any form of life. But God does nothing in vain. He always
has a purpose.

Apparently all such planets in the entire universe NOW are

waste and empty—decayed (*tohu* and *bohu*)—like the Earth was, as described in Genesis 1:2. But God did not create them in such conditions of decay—like our moon. Decay is *not* an original created condition—it is a condition *resulting from a process* of deterioration. Evidently if the now-fallen angels had maintained the Earth in its original beautiful condition, improved it, carried out God's instructions, and obeyed His government, they would have been offered the awesome potential of populating and carrying out a tremendous creative program throughout the entire universe. When they turned traitor on Earth, their sin must have also brought simultaneously physical destruction to the other planets throughout the universe, which were potentially and conditionally put in subjection to them.

As God surveyed this cataclysmic tragedy, He must have realized that since the highest, most perfect being within His almighty power to create, had turned to rebellion, it left God Himself as the only being who *would not* and *cannot* sin.

And God is the Father of the divine God Family.

Notice John 1:1-5. The "Word" who was "made flesh" (verse 14) has existed always—from eternity—with the Father. God the Father has created all things—the entire universe—by Him who became Jesus Christ (Ephesians 3:9; Colossians 1:16-17).

When Jesus was on Earth, He prayed to God, His Father in heaven. The Father spoke of Jesus as "my beloved son, in whom I am well pleased." Jesus lived on Earth as a human, tempted in all points as we are, yet without sin.

The fourth word in all the Bible is "God" (Genesis 1:1). And the original Hebrew word is "Elohim," a noun plural in form, like the word family, church, or group. The family is God. There is one God—the one Family, but more than one Person.

God saw that no being less than God, in the God Family, could be *certainly* relied on never to sin—to be like God—who cannot sin. To fulfill His purpose for the entire vast universe, God saw that nothing less than Himself (as the God Family) could be absolutely relied upon to carry out that supreme purpose in the entire universe.

God then purposed *to reproduce Himself*, through humans, made in His image and likeness, but made first from material flesh and blood, subject to death if there is sin unrepented of—yet with the possibility of being born into the divine Family begotten by God the Father.

God saw how this could be done through Christ, who gave Himself for that purpose.

And that is why God put man on the Earth! That is what caused God to do this most colossal, tremendous thing ever undertaken by the supreme, Almighty God—to reproduce Himself! The following chapter will make this undeniably clear.

Chapter 5
What Led to the Creation of MAN?

SOMETHING CAUSED THE CREATOR GOD TO DECIDE TO CREATE MAN on this planet. Few indeed know what it was and what the PURPOSE for humanity's presence really is. WHERE are we going, and what is *the way*?

These are the most vital questions. Yet, I repeat still again, science cannot give the answers. No religion has the explanation. No university teaches this most important of all knowledge.

EARTH NOT ORIGINALLY POPULATED BY MAN

Most people know almost nothing about God. To understand *ourselves*, WHY we are, where we are going, and how, we need to know more about our Creator.

Our present life is like going on a journey. Suppose you had just won a prize—an all-expense-paid trip to some other country. Wouldn't you want to know *where* you are going, how to get there, and as many things as possible about this trip? Should we not, then, be even more filled with eager anticipation to know as much as possible about this one *great* trip of life? And to know that, you need to know some things about the God who is sending you and providing the way.

It is vital at this point, then, to know this—as revealed in the Bible: The Eternal God not only is Creator of all that is, but is the RULER over all He creates and also EDUCATOR—that is, the Revealer of basic knowledge. He *reveals* knowledge basic and vital to know—knowledge otherwise inaccessible to man. Yet mankind—generally—has rejected revelation as a source of basic knowledge.

What God creates He *maintains*. What He creates He creates for a PURPOSE. He intends it to be put to *use*—a *right* use that *preserves and improves*. This use, maintenance and improvement is controlled in the process of united, cooperative action, by the GOVERNMENT OF GOD.

This Earth, originally, was intended to be the abode of a third of all the angels. The angels, beholding the Earth at its creation, found it so beautiful and perfect they shouted spontaneously for JOY! (Job 38:4-7). It was to provide a glorious opportunity for them. They were to work it, produce from it, and preserve and increase its beauty.

And at this point, it is well to understand the nature of God's original creation: It is like the unfinished furniture available in some stores. This furniture is "in the raw"—it is finished all but for the final varnish, polish, or paint. Some can save money by doing this *finishing* themselves—provided they have the skill to do so. This furniture may be of fine and superb quality—yet lacking the final beautifying *completion*.

So it is with God's creation. It is *perfect,* but subject to a beautifying finish which God intended angels to accomplish. The original "unfinished" creation was produced by God *alone*. But He intended angels, prehistorically, and MAN, now, to utilize creative power—to finish this part in God's creation—of adding the final beautifying and utilitarian phases of what shall be the FINAL COMPLETED CREATION!

And whether or not it had been revealed to the angels, it was a supreme TRIAL AND TEST. It was to be the PROVING GROUND of obedience to GOD'S GOVERNMENT and their fitness to develop into final finished creation the millions of other planets in the vast universe. For what is revealed in God's Word indicates that God had created the entire PHYSICAL universe at the same time He created the Earth. The seventh word in Genesis 1:1 should be translated "heavens."

Radioactive elements and the law of radioactivity prove that there was a time when MATTER did not exist. GOD is a spirit. God is composed of spirit. God was before ALL ELSE—the CREATOR of all. Angels were created prior to the Earth. What God reveals strongly implies that matter had never existed before the original creation of the Earth—that the entire *physical* universe was brought into being at that time.

So the angel potential was to take over the entire universe—to improve and finish the billions of physical planets surrounding the uncountable stars, many of which are SUNS. The sun in our solar system is merely an average-size sun. Some which we see as stars are actually many, many times larger than our sun. Our solar system, vast beyond the imagination of most minds, is only a *part* of our galaxy, and there are many galaxies! In other words, the physical UNIVERSE which the mighty God created is *vast beyond imagination!* How GREAT is the GREAT GOD!

He intended angels, and now MAN, to have a vital part in the final creation of the endless universe!

(But God may not have then fully revealed this awesome potential to the angels, for one third of them set out to take it from Him by force, without first qualifying.)

For this far-reaching purpose, God established His GOVERNMENT on Earth over them. The administration of the GOVERNMENT OF GOD over this globe was delegated to the super-archangel—the great cherub Lucifer.

Lucifer was the supreme masterpiece it was possible for even the great God to create as an individually created entity. The Bible reveals the existence of just two others of the same rank—Michael and Gabriel.

Bear in mind that even the holy angels and archangels—including this super cherub Lucifer—of necessity were endowed with ability to think, to reason, to form attitudes, and to make choices and decisions.

God started this Lucifer out with everything going for him. He sealed up the sum of wisdom, beauty and perfection. He was PERFECT in all his ways from the instant he was created UNTIL (Ezekiel 28:15) INIQUITY—rebellion, lawlessness—was found in him.

He had been trained and was thoroughly experienced in administration of the GOVERNMENT OF GOD at the very throne of the endless UNIVERSE! He was one of the two cherubs

whose wings covered the throne of God the Most High
(Ezekiel 28:14; Exodus 25:20).

He was created gloriously beautiful—*perfect* in beauty, but
he allowed vanity to seize him. Then he turned to erroneous
reasoning. God's LAW—the basis of God's government—is the
way of LOVE—outgoing concern for the good and welfare of
others, love toward God in obedience, humility and worship—
the way of giving, sharing, helping, cooperating. He reasoned
that competition would be better than cooperation. It would
be an incentive to excel, to try harder, to accomplish. There
would be more pleasure in serving SELF and more enjoyment.

He turned *against* God's law of LOVE. He became jealous of
God, envious, and resentful against God. He allowed lust and
greed to fill him, and he became bitter. This inspired a spirit
of *violence!* He deliberately became his Maker's adversary and
enemy. That was *his* choice, not God's—yet allowed by God!

God changed his NAME to what he became, SATAN the
DEVIL—which *means* adversary, competitor, enemy.

He directed his supernatural powers henceforth to EVIL. He
became bitter not only against God, but against God's LAW. He
used his subtle wiles of deception to lead the angels under
him into disloyalty, rebellion, and revolt against the Creator
and finally into a WAR of aggression and violence to attempt to
depose God and seize the throne of the UNIVERSE.

As long as Lucifer remained loyal and administered the GOV-
ERNMENT OF GOD faithfully, this Earth was filled with wonderful
and perfect PEACE. The angels were vigorously HAPPY to the
extent of JOY! The LAW of God's government is THE WAY OF LIFE
that CAUSES and produces peace, happiness, prosperity and well-
being. Sin is the WAY OF LIFE that has *caused* all existing EVILS.

The penalty of sin by the angels was *not* death—for God
had made them immortal spirit beings who cannot die. What
God gave them was THIS EARTH as their abode and opportunity
to qualify to possess and beautify the entire UNIVERSE.

Their penalty (they are still awaiting final judgment up to
now) was disqualification—forfeiture of their grand opportunity, perversion of mind, and *a colossal Earthwide CATACLYSM*
of destruction wreaked upon this Earth.

As a result, the Earth came to the condition briefly
described in Genesis 1:2—(the Hebrew words "tohu and bohu"

here mean waste and empty, chaotic and in extreme confusion) with water covering the whole face of the Earth, in deep darkness. Lucifer was created a perfect bringer of LIGHT. Now he became author of DARKNESS, error, confusion and evil.

So the rebellion of the angels that sinned (2 Peter 2:4-6; Jude 6-7; Isaiah 14:12-15; Ezekiel 28:12-17) brought this extreme cataclysm to the Earth.

And in all probability it did more!

Whatever God creates is created in perfect condition. The other planets were not created as dead hulks of waste and empty DECAY—like our moon and Mars. We do not yet know too much about the other planets, but every evidence so far indicates this same state of decay.

We have already covered the awesome, incredible POTENTIAL OF MAN. Originally, this potential of being put over the UNIVERSE was the potential of the angels. But they disqualified themselves.

God did not create our moon and the planets in this state of waste and decay. The evidence of what God does reveal strongly indicates that the entire material universe was created when the Earth was created. As just stated, God is NOT the author of waste, decay and destruction, but Satan is. It seems, therefore, based on what is *now revealed*, that a similar cataclysm of destruction most likely happened to the surface of our moon and the planets at the time it happened to this Earth! And all this was caused by the rebellion of Lucifer and his angels! But notice what God did next.

In Psalm 104:30, "Thou sendest forth thy spirit, they are created: and thou renewest the face of the earth."

Back, now, to Genesis 1:2, "And the earth was [became] without form, and void [Heb. *tohu* and *bohu*—chaotic, in confusion, waste and empty]; and darkness was upon the face of the deep. And the Spirit of God moved upon the face of the waters."

God now RENEWED the face of the Earth, preparing it to become the abode of *MAN!*

But *WHY?*

WHY GOD CREATED MAN!

Here is a truth perhaps never before understood by man!
Here is *AWESOME TRUTH!*

Look, now, at the situation as God must have seen and considered it. God has given us minds *like* the mind of God—only inferior and limited. God made us in His image, after His likeness (form and shape), only composed of matter instead of spirit. But God says to us, "Let this MIND be in you, which was also in Christ Jesus" (Philippians 2:5). We can learn to think His thoughts after Him. If we have His Spirit, we can learn to think, to some degree, even as HE THINKS!

How must God have looked at this situation after the colossal debacle of Lucifer and the angels that sinned?

This LUCIFER was the supreme MASTERPIECE of God's creative power as a single, separately created spirit being! He was created the most perfect in beauty, mentality, knowledge, power, intellect and wisdom within the almighty power of God to create in a being, with power to think, reason, make choices and decisions on his own. God knew that no higher, more perfect being could be created as an initial creation.

Yet this superior being, trained and experienced at the very throne of the GOVERNMENT OF GOD over the universe, had resorted to wrong reasoning and made a diabolical perverted decision. He worked on the angels under him until he turned their minds to rebellion also. This, incidentally, might have taken Lucifer millions of years. In all probability he had to begin perverting the minds of his angels one at a time, at first. He had to cause them to feel dissatisfied, wronged by God, and inject into them resentment and bitterness.

When Lucifer allowed thoughts of vanity, jealousy, envy, lust and greed, then resentment and rebellion, to enter and occupy his mind, SOMETHING HAPPENED TO HIS MIND! *His mind became perverted, distorted, twisted!* His thinking became warped. God gave him and the angels control over their own minds. They can never straighten them out—never again think rationally, honestly, rightly.

I have had a number of personal experiences with demons through a few demon-possessed people. I have cast out demons through the name of Christ and power of the Holy Spirit. Some demons are silly, like spoiled children. Some are crafty, sharp, shrewd, subtile. Some are belligerent, some are sassy, some are sullen and morose. But *all* are perverted, warped, twisted.

Look, now, again at God's overall supreme *PURPOSE*. It is to develop GODLY, PERFECT CHARACTER IN THE MILLIONS OF MAN-KIND WHO SHALL DO THIS CREATIVE COMPLETION THROUGHOUT THE ENTIRE LIMITLESS PHYSICAL UNIVERSE!

That is THE AWESOME PURPOSE!

For this PURPOSE, God started by creating millions of angels—spirit beings. Then He created the PHYSICAL UNIVERSE and this Earth, and He put angels here to develop this Earth, ruled by THE GOVERNMENT OF GOD.

But the king He set as ruler—LUCIFER—rebelled, revolted, misled a third of all the angels, and THE GOVERNMENT OF GOD no longer governed the Earth.

Lucifer was the supreme masterpiece. If Lucifer and his angels went wrong, there was no assurance the other two thirds would not.

As God surveyed this tragic cataclysm, He must have realized it left HIMSELF as the *ONLY* BEING who will not *and CANNOT SIN!* The only possible ASSURANCE of accomplishing His great PURPOSE was for Him now *to reproduce Himself!*

But let us answer another question before proceeding:

WHY is it IMPOSSIBLE for God to sin? No greater power exists that will prevent Him—but God has simply by His own power—supreme and above all power—set Himself that He *will not!*

What God saw was this. *No being less than God* could be *certainly* relied upon NEVER to sin, that is, NEVER to turn against God's LAW, and God's government, which makes possible His ultimate PURPOSE. To fulfill His PURPOSE for the entire UNIVERSE, God saw that nothing less than HIMSELF, and His holy, righteous and perfect CHARACTER, could be *absolutely relied upon* to carry out His SUPREME PURPOSE throughout the entire, vast, endless UNIVERSE!

The question might be raised: Could not God have known, in advance, what Lucifer and the angels under him would do? Doesn't God know EVERYTHING? The answer is NO. If God were to have known in advance what choice they would make, He would have had to FORCE them to make it—taken away from them power to think, to reason, to have a choice, to make deci-sions. God does not CHOOSE to know, in advance, what YOU or I will be thinking, reasoning, deciding, tomorrow or in the future. He gave these spirit beings, as He gives us, the power to think for ourselves, to choose, to make decisions. Otherwise we should be nothing more than automatons, doing what we are compelled to do. He simply did not *choose* to know. His PURPOSE includes the development of CHARACTER in His created beings.

All that had happened caused God to now UNDERTAKE THE MOST STUPENDOUS CREATION OF ALL—*that of REPRODUCING HIMSELF!* The ultimate creation of God beings in His God Family—superior to angels!

REPRODUCING HIMSELF??

Now came the *CROWNING PINNACLE* of even God's unmatched creative POWER! Now came the very zenith of all divine accomplishment! Now came a project so *incredulously transcendently* AWESOME it is hard for the human mind to grasp.

How could *the great GOD*—self-existent, *before* all else, CREATOR of all else, reproduce HIMSELF into multiplied *millions* of others JUST LIKE HIMSELF—divine, supreme in power, perfect in character—each by his own choice *perfectly* like-minded with the Father, each having so set himself that he CANNOT SIN?

The next chapter will reveal HOW God planned to carry out this incredibly AWESOME feat of *reproducing Himself.*

Chapter 6
HOW God Planned to Reproduce Himself!

I HAVE COVERED THE REASON *WHY* GOD DECIDED TO CREATE MAN and put the human family on the Earth. But *HOW* could so AWESOME an undertaking ever be brought about?

Few, indeed, have the slightest concept of what was involved. Few humans today have the slightest realization of the magnitude of miraculous occurrences and divine planning required so that this HUMAN LIFE each of us enjoys could be made possible.

In the previous chapter I mentioned that the question might be asked, "Could not God have known, in advance, what Lucifer would do?" The answer was NO! But assuredly God *did know* Lucifer's rebellion and the sin of the angels on Earth was a *possibility*.

And, knowing of that possibility, did God wait until after that Earthwide cataclysm occurred before any thought of creating MAN entered His mind? And again the answer is a definite *NO!* He did *not* wait until that tragic cataclysm to begin planning the reproduction of His own kind.

Let me give an illustration. I fly in a Gulfstream-II jet aircraft. Its human designers realized the *possibility* of different *parts* or systems failing. So they designed and installed what is called a "fail-safe" system. If a certain part goes wrong, another part or system takes over immediately—and in some cases, even a third part or system. If human designers plan ahead *in case* of a mechanical failure, how much more would the GREAT

CREATOR GOD have planned ahead in the event Lucifer and the angels sinned! Undoubtedly God planned ahead. He knew, before the creation of the Earth, that angels, with independent powers of thinking, reasoning, choosing, forming opinions and decisions, *could* rebel and turn to iniquity. His great PURPOSE required Him to allow this!

Perhaps that was a reason why He created MATTER—the entire physical universe. Matter, with its many properties—such as organic and inorganic matter, force, energy, inertia, gravity, etc.—provided material by which He could form MAN in a mortal state, as the means by which He might reproduce Himself.

At this point, we need to KNOW STILL MORE about our Creator GOD! And we need to know WHY almost *no one* today has had the faintest idea of such a colossal, supremely AWESOME project going on!

ONLY ONE GOD—MORE THAN ONE PERSON!

Let me try to make this most wonderful truth of all time PLAIN!

First, go back once again to the very first words in God's revelation of knowledge to us: "In the beginning *God* created the heavens and the earth."

God inspired Moses to write those words in Hebrew, not in the English words above. I repeat, the Hebrew name translated "God" is *Elohim*—a noun plural in form, like the words *family, church, group, team. One* family, but composed of more than one person. ONE church, but composed of more than one member. ONE group, but unless composed of more than one person, it would not be a group. *One* athletic team, but composed of two, five, six, nine, eleven or more players—besides a number of substitutes.

This former Lucifer, who became Satan, has so cleverly DECEIVED all humanity that almost no one today knows that God is, actually, *a divine FAMILY. One* Family. God IS a Family. That Family *is* ONE GOD.

Satan has deceived people into almost every other belief. Perhaps the largest number have been deceived into believing God is a "trinity"—God in THREE persons—LIMITING God to three persons and misrepresenting the HOLY SPIRIT, which flows from God and from Christ, to be a single person.

Others think of God as ONE PERSON *ONLY*.

But notice, again, in the New Testament, John 1:1-5, 14:

"In the beginning was the Word...." Sounds similar to Genesis 1:1, doesn't it? In Genesis 1:1, it is: "In the beginning God ...." But the English name GOD in Genesis 1:1 is translated from the Hebrew *Elohim,* meaning more than one person forming *ONE God.* In John 1, the word "Word" in English is translated from the original inspired Greek word *logos,* which means "word," "spokesman," "revelatory thought," as a being or person.

The next words in John 1, "...and the Word was with God, and the Word was God. The same was in the beginning with God. All things were made by him; and without him was not any thing made that was made" (verses 1-3).

This "Logos" was a person. This person existed "from the beginning" the same as God. He *ALWAYS* self-existed. He existed *with* God. And He, also, *was* God. He is and was a Person. God, whom He was WITH, is also a Person. They both coexisted forever. "All things" (words elsewhere translated "the universe") were made by Him—the Word—the divine Spokesman.

But now notice verse 14: "And the Word was made flesh, and dwelt among us, (and we beheld his glory, the glory as of the only begotten of the Father,) full of grace and truth." This, of course, is speaking of Jesus Christ. In the human flesh, He was begotten of God the Father, the *only* one ever so begotten (before human birth).

At the time of this begettal and human birth "the Word" *became* the Son of God.

The Father, from heaven, said of Jesus, "Thou art my beloved *Son,* in whom I am well pleased." Jesus, praying, called God "Father"—Father and Son—a FAMILY relationship. The Church, at the resurrection to immortal SPIRIT life, is to MARRY the resurrected and glorified Christ (Ephesians 5:25-28). So we have here a FAMILY relationship—father, son, husband and wife. And the "wife" is to be composed of *born children of God.*

I personally have been the father of a FAMILY. My family name is Armstrong. My first wife and I lived together 50 years until her death. I have a son, Garner Ted. My son is also ARMSTRONG, just as Jesus, the Word, was God, and yet He was *with* God. Our family name is Armstrong. All members of the family also were named Armstrong. When our daughters married, they started each the forming of another family, and they took the name of the husband who became the father of *that* family. But each family is only ONE family.

Likewise, there is but *ONE* God—but God is the family name, and there is *more than one person* in the *ONE* Family.

CHRIST THE MAKER OF ALL

God is Creator. But God is the divine Family. How can the Father of the Family be Creator, and Christ also Creator? In Ephesians 3:9 it is written that God the Father "created all things [the universe] by Jesus Christ." And Christ is "the Word"—the Spokesman. Speaking of Him, we read in Psalm 33, "By *the word* of the [Eternal] were the heavens [universe] made; and all the host of them by the breath of his mouth.... For he spake, and it was done ..." (verses 6, 9).

I will illustrate. In January 1914, I was sent by a national magazine to interview Henry Ford in Detroit. When I first saw him, he was just outside the door of the huge Ford factory. He was wearing a business suit, not workman's overalls. He was the maker, or manufacturer, of the Ford cars. He made them BY his thousands of employees, whom I saw in overalls at work inside the factory. The employees used machinery and the power of electricity. Likewise, God the Father is Creator. He created BY Jesus Christ, the "workman" who spake, and it was done by the power of the Holy Spirit. But Jesus said plainly that He "spake" only as the Father commanded Him.

Notice Colossians 1: Speaking of the Father (verse 12) and "his dear Son" (verse 13), "[w]ho is the image of the invisible God ... For by him [Christ] were all things [the universe] created, that are in heaven, and that are in earth, visible and invisible, whether they be thrones, or dominions, or principalities, or powers: all things were created by him, and for him: And he is before all things, and by him all things consist" (verses 15-17).

Jesus Christ, prior to human birth, had existed with the Father—always, eternally!

JUST HOW DID GOD PLAN TO REPRODUCE HIMSELF?

From eternity the Father and the WORD, who became Jesus Christ, had co-existed. They had created angels—probably many millions of them. A third of them, under Lucifer, were put on the Earth at its creation. God set His GOVERNMENT over them, with Lucifer on the throne. Lucifer rejected God's government. He and the angels became DISQUALIFIED—the GOVERNMENT OF GOD was no longer being administered on Earth—and the Earth had become waste, empty, in decay, and in darkness.

Were there, prior to this, more than just the TWO—God and the Word—in the GOD FAMILY? God reveals no more. Was the "Word" the Son of God, and was God His Father *at that time?* They are nowhere referred to as that.

To have been the Son of God at that prehistoric time, God would of necessity have existed *prior* to the Son's birth. The Son, had that been the case, would have *come into* existence at time of such birth. But the "Logos"—the Word—had, like God, eternally *self*-existed.

Consider, now, the truly AWESOME project God set out to accomplish—to REPRODUCE HIMSELF!

It is probable that, prior to this time, no form of life had ever been created with the reproductive process. Probably the very first example of reproductive life was that of plant life—at the time God was *renewing* the face of the Earth (Genesis 1:11-12).

God had created the physical universe before placing the angels on the Earth. God had created MATTER containing properties so that marvelous things may be done with it. There is both organic (living) and inorganic (inert—dead) matter. In matter are such properties as energy, gravity, inertia. Awesome powers, such as the hydrogen bomb, may come from it. The existence of MATTER offered God what He needed to reproduce Himself. After creation of reproductive plant life, God created animal life with the reproductive process, each reproducing after its own kind—cattle after the cattle kind, horses after the horse kind, etc.

But now God (*Elohim*) said, "Let *us* make man in *our* image, after *our* likeness [form, shape] ..." (Genesis 1:26); in other words, AFTER THE GOD KIND.

God had created angels out of SPIRIT. But now, for His own reproductive purpose, MATTER offered God the properties He needed.

And so "…the [ETERNAL] God formed man of the dust of the ground"—out of MATTER (Genesis 2:7).

IF AND WHEN MAN SINNED

At this point we must consider a basic principle of GOD'S GOVERNMENT. The state can never be without a head. God placed Lucifer on the throne of the Earth. He was no longer administering the GOVERNMENT OF GOD—he was now disqualified—but he (his name now changed to Satan) must remain on that throne until his successor has qualified *and* also been inducted into office. The very *fact* that Satan was there to tempt the first humans—that he is, even now, "the god of this world" (2 Corinthians 4:4) and "the prince of the power of the air" (Ephesians 2:2)—is sufficient evidence of this basic principle of the GOVERNMENT OF GOD.

More than this, once the Earth became inhabited *by* those in rebellion against the government of God—once that government ceased to function—it became necessary for someone to qualify as successor to Lucifer (now Satan)—and in order to qualify to *restore* the government and WAY of God, the successor *must* actually *reject* and/or turn from Satan's WAY!

More, those who are to reign WITH Christ, must also qualify by turning from or rejecting Satan's way, *overcoming* that way, and actually living *under the* WAY of God's law.

Knowing this, God knew the inevitability that Satan would tempt the first created MAN to disbelieve God and commit sin. If the super-archangel and all his angels had been led into rebellion, how much more certain that man, made lower than the angels, would also sin!

Can you visualize God and with Him the Word (also God—of the God FAMILY) planning this supreme feat of their creative power? The Word volunteered to give up temporarily the supreme POWER and GLORY He had possessed always (John 17:5), to divest Himself of all that, to be begotten by God, born in human flesh for the purpose of death (Hebrews 2:9). Since God delegated the actual MAKING of man to the Word, He, *when* physically born as a human being, for the *purpose* of death, would, *in* that death, be giving a life of greater value than the sum total of ALL HUMAN LIVES—since He was their MAKER. And, being DIVINE as well as human—being God as well as man, He in the person of Christ, would be able to *avoid* sinning. Then He, who NEVER sinned, although tempted in all points just like the rest of us humans, *in* death could PAY in our stead THE PENALTY WE HAVE INCURRED.

By creating MAN out of physical matter, being mortal, man could DIE. So man's penalty for sin was DEATH. ("For the wages of sin is DEATH; but the GIFT of God is eternal life through Jesus Christ our Lord"—Romans 6:23.)

God the Father would have power to resurrect Christ to immortal life *from the dead*—thus making a resurrection to immortal spirit-composed life possible for humans.

So, God's master plan for accomplishing His PURPOSE took form and shape. IF man sinned—as all but Jesus have—it could thus be possible for him to REPENT—to turn FROM sinning to be reconciled to God and to live GOD'S WAY OF LIFE. In other words, to turn *to* the GOVERNMENT OF GOD, accept its rule over his life, accept Christ as his Savior and coming KING. And He, Christ, would qualify to REESTABLISH the GOVERNMENT OF GOD ON THE EARTH!

But what if sinning man *refused* to repent—to turn FROM Satan's way and to let the GOVERNMENT OF GOD rule in his life? Then there would be the *second* death for any or all such (Revelation 20:14)—when they would *cease to exist—be as if they had never been* (Obadiah 16).

But was this, that I have just covered above, all that God (in the persons of God AND THE WORD) had to consider? No. Far from it!

The plan was to make MAN out of physical substance. But how would God reproduce *Himself* or bring perhaps millions upon millions *into* the GOD FAMILY?

This necessitated that God's very own LIFE—divine GOD-life—be imparted. God IS a spirit—*composed* of spirit.

And yet this is made possible *only* after God's own holy, righteous and perfect CHARACTER has been wrought in each human—by that human's repentance and faith—during this earthly mortal life.

What a *marvelous* plan God conceived. He would form man of physical MATTER—so that, *if* man totally failed, he could be as though he had never been, could be destroyed. So God made man of PHYSICAL substance, formed and shaped like God so that man could be converted—changed from matter into spirit composition at a resurrection—a spirit-composed member of the GOD FAMILY.

Can your mind grasp what matchless wisdom, power of designing and planning, made our transcendent human potential possible?

God first formed PLANT life—the flora. This was living matter reproducing itself, but without self-consciousness—without brain. Next God created the fauna—animal life, in which He placed BRAIN, with a certain consciousness, yet without the thinking, reasoning, decision-making processes. But MAN, to be reproduced into the GOD FAMILY, was designed to have a GODLY-type MIND, ability to think, reason, make choices and decisions—develop God-like CHARACTER.

How could all this be done? Actually the brain of an elephant, a whale or a dolphin is virtually equal in complexity, design and quality and larger in size than human brain. The chimpanzee's is also virtually equal, but slightly smaller in size. WHY, then, is the human MIND so *transcendently superior* to animal brain?

Chapter 7
Bridging the Gap Between Human Man and the Ultimate Spirit-Composed Sons of God

A HUMAN MANUFACTURER SENDS ALONG WITH THE INSTRUMENT or device he manufactures an INSTRUCTION BOOKLET describing what his product is intended to do with full directions for accomplishing its purpose. The most perfect mechanism ever designed and made is the marvelous mind and body that is MAN. And it is also only natural that our Maker sent along His INSTRUCTION BOOK—revealing for our good what WE ARE, WHY we are, where we are going, and what is *the way*.

That instruction book is the Holy Bible. Yet man has made this the most MISunderstood, misinterpreted and maligned book that ever came into human hands.

Nevertheless, the MISSING DIMENSION IN KNOWLEDGE is all there revealed. The incredible HUMAN POTENTIAL is there revealed and made plain—if MAN would only read it—and BELIEVE WHAT IT SAYS!

That is our source book. It covers pre-history, history, instruction for the present, and prophecy revealing the future.

It reveals, as we have seen in preceding chapters, that originally from eternity, there existed GOD and with Him there coexisted, also from eternity, "THE WORD," a second PERSON who also is God. God created all things by and through this coexisting SPIRIT BEING called "THE WORD" (John 1:1-4).

In Genesis 1:1, the Hebrew word translated "God" is *Elohim*, a noun or name, plural in form, meaning ONE GOD who is composed of *more than one person*. In other words, *a divine FAMILY,* of which the GOD mentioned in John 1:1 is HEAD.

We have seen how the Bible reveals that God first created angels—also composed of spirit, though lesser beings than God, and lacking in creative power.

Next, God created—brought into existence—the physical universe, including the Earth. At Earth's creation, a third of the angels were placed here. They were put under rule of the GOVERNMENT OF GOD, administered by the great archangel Lucifer, a cherub. Under the GOVERNMENT OF GOD the Earth was filled with wonderful PEACE, HAPPINESS and JOY. But ultimately Lucifer led his angels into rebellion. The GOVERNMENT OF GOD was rejected, no longer enforced. The Earth, as a result, became waste and empty, in confusion and utter darkness.

Then in six days God renewed the face of the Earth. During this "creation week" of Genesis 1, God formed the first life forms that reproduced themselves—the flora and then the fauna—without the thinking, reasoning, decision-making process, and without ethical, moral or spiritual capabilities.

Finally came the creation of MAN—created in God's own image and likeness—form and shape—but like animals composed of physical MATTER from the earth. MAN, to be born ultimately into the very GOD FAMILY, was designed to have GODLY-type MIND—ability to think, to reason, to make choices and decisions, capable of forming ethical, moral and spiritual attitudes.

Remember, God's PURPOSE in creating man is to reproduce Himself—with such perfect spiritual CHARACTER as ONLY GOD possesses—who WILL NOT and therefore CANNOT ever SIN! (1 John 3:9).

Such perfect spiritual and holy character *cannot* be created by fiat. It must be *developed,* and that requires TIME and EXPERIENCE.

Such character—I repeat—is the ability in a single entity to come to comprehend and distinguish the true values from the false, the right way from the wrong, to choose the right and reject the wrong, and, with power of WILL, to *DO* the right and resist the evil.

Animals are equipped with BRAIN and instinct. But they do not have power to understand and choose moral and spiritual values or to develop perfect spiritual CHARACTER. Animals have BRAIN, but no intellect—instinct, but no ability to develop HOLY and GODLY CHARACTER.

And that pictures the transcendental DIFFERENCE between animal BRAIN and human MIND.

But WHAT CAUSES that vast difference?

There is virtually no difference in shape and construction between animal brain and human brain. The brains of elephants, whales and dolphins are larger than human brain, and the chimp's brain is slightly smaller. Qualitatively the human brain may be very slightly superior, but not enough to remotely account for the difference in output.

What, then, can account for the vast difference? Science cannot adequately answer. Some scientists, in the field of brain research, conclude that, of necessity, there has to be some nonphysical component in human brain that does not exist in animal brain. But most scientists will not admit the possibility of the existence of the nonphysical.

What other explanation is there? Actually, outside of the very slight degree of physical superiority of human brain, science has NO explanation, due to unwillingness to concede even the possibility of the spiritual.

When man refuses to admit even the very existence of his own Maker, he shuts out of his mind vast oceans of basic true knowledge, fact, and UNDERSTANDING. When he substitutes FABLE for truth, he is, of all men, MOST IGNORANT, though he professes himself to be wise.

When man, in the name of science, denies—or by indifference, ignores—his Maker, he blinds his mind to what he is, why he is, where he is going, and what is THE WAY! No wonder this world is filled with evils! There has to be a CAUSE for every effect!

But when our minds are opened to the knowledge of our GOD and His purposes, then we have glorious access to the vast MISSING DIMENSION OF KNOWLEDGE: the very knowledge that God is the divine FAMILY—that God is REPRODUCING HIMSELF—

that He is using MATTER in the process, and that He opens our understanding to vast vistas of new knowledge.

So now CONSIDER. God is composed of SPIRIT. God is CREATOR, DESIGNER, RULER, EDUCATOR. God has SUPREME MIND. He IS the PERFECT HOLY AND RIGHTEOUS CHARACTER!

But He is using material substance from this physical earth with which to REPRODUCE HIMSELF. Out of physical EARTH He has formed MAN in His image and likeness (form and shape).

But if man is to BECOME God, in the process of God reproducing Himself, then the CHARACTER that is to be built in him MUST emanate from God—and the spirit LIFE that is to be his also must emanate from GOD.

In other words, God has had to plan to *bridge the gap* between MATTER (of which MAN is now wholly composed) and SPIRIT (which God now is, and man must become).

Matter is *NOT* spirit—cannot be converted into spirit. *HOW*, then, can God change mortal material MAN into immortal, spirit-composed GOD?

Man is composed *wholly* of MATTER. God says: "And the [Eternal] God formed man of the dust of the ground, and breathed into his nostrils the breath of life; and man became a living soul" (Genesis 2:7). MAN was made out of the dust of the ground. He receives his temporary human life from air, breathed in and out of his nostrils. His *life* is in the blood (Genesis 9:4, 6). But the lifeblood is oxidized by breathing air, even as gasoline in the carburetor of an automobile. Therefore breath is the "breath of life" even as the life is in the blood.

Notice carefully that MAN, made wholly of matter, BECAME a *living soul* as soon as the BREATH gave him his temporary physical life. The scripture does NOT say "immortal" soul. Man does not *have* an "immortal" soul. He IS a soul as soon as physical LIFE enters him.

The Hebrew word for "soul" is *nephesh*. In Genesis 1:20-24, animals are called *nephesh* three times—only the translators translated the Hebrew word there *"creature."* Animals have the same temporary physio-chemical existence as man. Both die the same death (Ecclesiastes 3:19-20).

"[T]he soul that sinneth, it shall die" (Ezekiel 18:4). Again, God's Word says: "The soul that sinneth, it shall die" (verse 20). Adam was a soul, and God said to him, in regard to the tree of the knowledge of good and evil, "…in the day that thou eatest thereof thou shalt surely die" (Genesis 2:17). But Satan denied this, and Adam and Eve believed Satan, as most of humanity has done ever since.

So let us UNDERSTAND! Man is FLESH and BLOOD—composed wholly of MATTER—and that living matter *IS* a living soul.

The SOUL is composed of physical MATTER, not spirit.

I have explained that human brain is almost identical to animal brain. But man was made in the form and shape of God, to have a special relationship with God—to have the potential of being born into the FAMILY of God. And God is SPIRIT (John 4:24).

To make it possible to *bridge the gap*—or to make the transition of MANKIND, composed wholly of MATTER, into SPIRIT beings in God's Kingdom, then to be composed wholly of spirit, and at the same time to give MAN a MIND like God's—God put *a spirit* in each human.

In Job 32:8, we read, "[T]here is a spirit in man: and the inspiration of the Almighty giveth them understanding."

This is a great TRUTH, understood by but very few.

I call this spirit the HUMAN spirit, for it is *IN* each human, even though it is SPIRIT ESSENCE and not matter. It is NOT a spirit *person* or being. It is not the MAN, but spirit essence *IN* the man. It is NOT a *soul*—the physical human is a soul. The human spirit imparts the power of INTELLECT to the human brain. The human spirit does not supply human LIFE—the human LIFE is in the physical BLOOD, oxidized by the BREATH of life.

It is that nonphysical component in the human brain that *does not* exist in the brain of animals. It is the ingredient that makes possible the transition from human to divine, *without* changing matter *into* spirit, at the time of resurrection. That I will explain a little later.

Let me make clear a few essential points about this spirit in man. It is spirit essence, just as in matter air is essence, and so is water. This human spirit cannot see. The physical BRAIN sees, through the eyes. The human spirit IN a person cannot hear. The brain hears through the ears. This human spirit cannot think. The brain thinks—although the spirit imparts the power to think, whereas brute animal brains without such spirit cannot, except in the most elementary manner.

A scripture often used by believers in an "immortal soul" explains. In 1 Corinthians 2, the Apostle Paul is explaining to the Corinthians that he did not come to them using hard-to-understand speech as many do to exalt their own vanity. He came to them with plain and simple speech, in humility. And yet none of the princes, the elite, the highly educated—the rulers—of this world could understand.

WHY couldn't the more highly learned understand? Because he was preaching Christ's message of the Kingdom of God. This is *spiritual* knowledge. This kind of knowledge cannot be seen by the physical eye, nor heard with the physical ear. Spiritual knowledge cannot enter the human mind by natural means—for spirit cannot be seen, heard, felt, tasted or smelled.

Then he explains that in this manner (verse 11) no MAN could have the knowledge a man possesses, except by "the spirit of man which is in him." The brute animal has a brain virtually identical to human brain—and some even larger. But their brains cannot KNOW—comprehend—what man knows. Neither could man without the spirit of man which is in him. In other words, this spirit imparts the power of intellect to the human brain.

Yet this human MIND is limited to knowledge of the physical. It cannot KNOW—comprehend—the spiritual things of God. WHY? Because even the human MIND only can know, naturally, what knowledge comes to it through the senses of seeing, hearing, smelling, tasting, feeling. A brute animal also may see, hear, smell, taste or feel what a man does, and still be unable to utilize what enters his brain in thought or knowledge. The reason for this will be explained later.

Now the second half of 1 Corinthians 2:11: "[E]VEN SO" (in like manner) no man can know—have knowledge of, understand or comprehend—the things of GOD, except by ANOTHER spirit, *the Holy Spirit of GOD.*

Just as no dumb animal can know the things of man's knowledge, neither could man, by brain alone, except by the spirit of man—the human spirit—that is in man. So also, in the same manner, even a man cannot know—comprehend— the things of God, unless or until he receives *another* spirit— *the Holy Spirit of GOD.*

Stated still another way, all humans have from conception a spirit called "the spirit of man" which is IN THEM. Notice carefully that this spirit is NOT the man. It is something *IN THE MAN*. A man might swallow a small marble. It is then something *in* the man, but it is *not* the man or any part of him as a man. The man was made of the dust of the ground—mortal. This human spirit is not the soul. It is something IN the soul which soul itself *IS* the physical MAN.

Notice, further, verse 14: "But the natural man receiveth not the things of the Spirit of God: for they are foolishness unto him: neither can he know them, because they are spiritually discerned."

So, from conception, God gives us one spirit, which for lack of a better term I call a human spirit. It gives us MIND power which is not in animal BRAIN. Yet that MIND power is *limited* to knowledge of the physical universe. WHY? Because knowledge enters the human mind ONLY through the five physical senses.

But notice that God had not completed the creation of MAN at the creation of Adam and Eve. The *physical* creation was completed. They had this "human" spirit at their creation.

But now must follow the spiritual creation. This required *a second* spirit in man—the HOLY SPIRIT of God.

"And the [Eternal] God formed man of the dust of the ground, and … planted a garden eastward in Eden; and there he put the man whom he had formed. And out of the ground made the [Eternal] God to grow every tree that is pleasant to the sight, and good for food; the tree of life also in the midst of the garden, and the tree of knowledge of good and evil" (Genesis 2:7-9).

Actually and literally, Adam, as yet, was "not all there." The spirit of man was in him—but not the Spirit of God. God offered him freely the fruit of the TREE OF LIFE—which symbolized God's HOLY SPIRIT. Taking of the tree of LIFE would have done two things: (1) opened his MIND to comprehend spiritual knowledge, and (2) imparted within him the GIFT of God's Holy Spirit, leading to ETERNAL LIFE. But, when God explained to him the KINGDOM OF GOD, Adam disbelieved what God said and disobeyed—SINNED. Then what?

"And the [Eternal] God said … and now, lest he put forth his hand, and take also of the tree of life, and eat, and live for ever:

Therefore the [Eternal] God sent him forth from the garden of Eden, to till the ground from whence he was taken. So he drove out the man; and he placed at the east of the garden of Eden Cherubims, and a flaming sword which turned every way, to keep the way of the tree of life" (Genesis 3:22-24).

Now GRASP THIS, please!

Do not forget God's great PURPOSE! Through human man, composed of material substance, God is reproducing Himself— adding to His own holy, righteous, sinless GOD FAMILY. But God is composed of SPIRIT. How does God *bridge the gap* between mortal physical MAN and immortal SPIRIT-composed God?

The *very first* human had made the wrong choice, and by SIN rejected the GOVERNMENT OF GOD. God then drove him out of the Garden of Eden and blocked all possible reentry to the tree of life. But of course God anticipated the probability of this. God's PURPOSE must STAND! But *HOW?*

It now required the "second Adam"—Jesus Christ. He had offered Himself before the world was. But He was not to come, born human for the purpose of death, for about another 4,000 years.

God had marked out a 7,000-year period—the first 6,000 for mankind, *cut off from God* (with a few exceptions), to go its own way—to write the lesson in human suffering and anguish of living *contrary* to GOD'S WAY OF LIFE, commanded by THE GOVERNMENT OF GOD—which Adam rejected.

This 6,000 years, with Satan still here, would be followed by a single 1,000 years, during which CHRIST would rule, having qualified to restore THE GOVERNMENT OF GOD on Earth. Satan would be totally restrained during the seventh millennium.

During that seventh millennium, the KINGDOM OF GOD— the RULING FAMILY OF GOD—would be established on Earth.

Meanwhile, during the first 6,000 years, a FEW would be offered opportunity to enter into the *spiritual creation*, which begins with the receiving of the SECOND SPIRIT—that is, the gift of the HOLY SPIRIT of God. Outside of this comparative few, God adopted a "hands-off" policy toward the human race. Abel, Adam's second son, apparently followed God's way, for Christ called him "righteous Abel." Enoch "walked with God." Noah found favor with God—but apparently that was all during the first 1,900 years or so.

After the Flood, Abraham, Isaac, Israel and Joseph lived God's way. Then God called and formed the nation of Israel, but they were offered no spiritual salvation or eternal life—only material and national blessings. God called and used a few prophets. Then Christ came and made spiritual salvation possible for all. Yet only the first comparatively very small spiritual harvest has been called to spiritual salvation during the nearly 2,000 years since Christ.

HUMAN REPRODUCTION THE TYPE OF GOD'S REPRODUCING HIMSELF

Few people realize that human reproduction has a sacred and GOD-PLANE MEANING NOT APPLICABLE TO ANY OTHER KIND OF LIFE.

Human reproduction pictures spiritual salvation—which is actually God the Father reproducing Himself in the GOD FAMILY.

Now see the ASTOUNDING COMPARISON!

MAN, remember, is composed wholly of MATTER from the ground (Genesis 2:7; 3:19). But HOW can God bridge the gap, in reproducing Himself, of converting a wholly physical man into a wholly spirit-composed member of the GOD FAMILY?

It *starts* with a spirit (a portion of spirit essence) IN the wholly physical man. Remember, this spirit is NOT the man—only something IN the man. Remember, too, this spirit cannot see, hear, or think. The MAN sees, hears and thinks through his physical brain and the five senses of seeing, hearing, tasting, smelling and feeling. The spirit in man imparts the power of PHYSICAL INTELLECT to the physical brain, thus forming human MIND.

This spirit acts, among other things, as a COMPUTER, adding to the brain the psychic and intellectual power. Knowledge received in the brain through the eye, ear, and the senses is immediately "programmed" into the spirit computer. All memory is stored in this spirit computer. This "computer" gives the brain *instant recall* of whatever portion of millions of bits of knowledge may be needed in the reasoning process. That is to say that MEMORY is recorded in the human spirit, whether or not it also is recorded in the "gray matter" of BRAIN.

This human spirit also adds to man a spiritual and moral faculty not possessed by animals.

God had made the needed second spirit—the HOLY SPIRIT—available to Adam. But on Adam's rebellion and taking the forbidden fruit, God had driven Adam out and closed all access to the tree of LIFE—symbolic of His Holy Spirit.

Yet through Christ, a repentant humanity may yet receive God's GIFT of His Holy Spirit. To Nicodemus Christ said, "Except a man be born again, he cannot see the kingdom of God." Of course Nicodemus could not quite understand that. Almost nobody today understands it. Jesus explained, "That which is born of the flesh IS FLESH; and that which is born of the Spirit IS SPIRIT" (John 3:6). Man came from the ground. He IS flesh. Jesus was not talking about another *physical* birth or experience of conversion in *this life*—but about a *spiritual* birth—when man shall BE spirit, no longer composed of matter, but composed wholly of SPIRIT! Yes, LITERALLY! Then he shall have been born of God. God is spirit (John 4:24, RSV).

Now to become human, each of us had to be *begotten* by his human father. Likewise, to be born *again*—of THE SPIRIT which is of GOD the Father, one must first be *begotten* of the SPIRITUAL FATHER—of GOD.

This is explained in Romans 8:16-17: "The Spirit [of God] itself beareth witness with our spirit, that we are the [begotten] children of God: And if children, then heirs [not yet inheritors or possessors]; heirs of God, and joint-heirs with Christ...."

And God's Holy Spirit, now combined with our human spirit in the human MIND, does two things: (1) begets the human with divine eternal life to be later BORN into the GOD FAMILY as a divine being, then composed wholly of spirit; (2) imparts to the human mind power to comprehend SPIRITUAL KNOWLEDGE—to understand the things of God (1 Corinthians 2:11). Also, God's Holy Spirit imparts divine LOVE, FAITH and POWER to overcome Satan and sin.

This Spirit-begotten Christian now has, conditionally, the PRESENCE OF ETERNAL LIFE—GOD LIFE—within him (or her), but is NOT YET an immortal SPIRIT BEING—not yet composed wholly of SPIRIT.

He is now an *heir* of God as the son of a wealthy man is the heir of his father—but NOT YET "born again"—NOT YET an inheritor or a possessor. But IF His Holy Spirit dwells in us, God will, at Christ's coming back to Earth as King of kings, "quicken" to immortality our mortal bodies BY His Spirit that dwells in us (Romans 8:11; 1 Corinthians 15:49-53).

Now see how the astonishing analogy continues:

Just as in human reproduction, the impregnated embryo, which later becomes the fetus, is not yet BORN, but still being nourished through the human mother; so the begotten Christian is *not yet* BORN into the God Family. The divine life has merely been begotten.

Satan has managed to deceive most of fundamentalist Christianity into believing they already are "born again" on accepting Christ.

But just as in human reproduction when the HUMAN characteristics of form and shape and the human body and brain gradually begin to form during the period of gestation, so now the RIGHTEOUS and HOLY CHARACTER of God begins to take form and GROW. Actually, in many, this divine CHARACTER may form so slowly it seems hardly in evidence at first, except that in some there will appear the glow of that ecstasy of spiritual "romance"—which may radiate in that "first love" of spiritual conversion. But, so far as growing in SPIRITUAL KNOWLEDGE (2 Peter 3:18) and spiritual CHARACTER goes, most of that is still to be learned and developed.

When newly converted, one is now a spiritual "EMBRYO." Now he must be nourished and fed on SPIRITUAL FOOD. Jesus said man must not live by bread (physical food) alone, but by EVERY WORD OF GOD. The BIBLE is the written Word of God, just as Christ is the personal Word of God. This growth is the character development that REQUIRES TIME and comes largely by EXPERIENCE.

Above all, it requires continual BIBLE STUDY to show ONE'S SELF approved of God, as well as much continual and earnest PRAYER. When you study the Bible, GOD IS TALKING TO YOU. When you PRAY, you are TALKING TO HIM. You get to really KNOW God in this manner, just as you become better acquainted with people by conversation.

Yet much of this spiritual character development comes through Christian fellowship with other spiritually begotten people in God's Church.

Further, just as the human physical embryo and fetus are given physical nourishment through the human mother, God's

CHURCH is the spiritual MOTHER of its members. God's Church is called "Jerusalem … above … which is the MOTHER of us all" (Galatians 4:26).

Notice the exact parallel. God has set called and chosen ministers in His Church to feed the flock, "For the perfecting of the saints, for THE WORK OF THE MINISTRY [proclaiming Christ's gospel of the Kingdom of God in all the world], for the edifying of the body [Church] of Christ: Till we all come in the unity of the faith, and of the knowledge of the Son of God, unto a perfect man, unto the measure of the stature of the fulness of Christ" (Ephesians 4:12-13).

It is the duty of Christ's true ministers (and how few today) to PROTECT the begotten but yet unborn saints from false doctrines and from false ministers!

What a wonderful picture of God's reproducing Himself is human reproduction!

And remember God intended human reproduction to be a FAMILY matter. It adds human children to the human FAMILY. The HUMAN FAMILY is the exact TYPE of the GOD FAMILY. God has bestowed MARRIAGE and FAMILY life on *NO OTHER* form of life except on HUMANS, whose potential it is to enter the FAMILY OF GOD!

But *consider further!* As the physical human fetus must grow *physically* large enough to be born, so the begotten Christian must grow *spiritually* in grace and knowledge of Christ (2 Peter 3:18)—must overcome, develop in spiritual character, during this life, to be born into the Kingdom of God!

That is well illustrated by the parables of the pounds and the talents. In the parable of the pounds (Luke 19:11-27), Jesus pictured Himself as a nobleman going to a far country (heaven) to receive a kingdom and later to return. He called his 10 servants and gave each a pound. While He was gone, one of the 10 traded with the money and gained 10 pounds. He was commended and made ruler over 10 cities in the Kingdom of God. A second gained only five pounds—he did half as well, starting with EQUAL ability. He was given reign over five cities. A third gained NOTHING—and had even that pound taken from him.

In the parable of the talents (Matthew 25:14-30), one was given five talents, another two talents, and another one—each according to his own ability (like handicap golf). On Christ's return, the one who had been given five talents had gained five more (representing spiritual growth and overcoming in this life). He was commended as a good and faithful servant and given responsibilities accordingly in God's Kingdom. The one who had gained another two accomplished just as much in proportion to ability. He, too, received an equal reward. But the one who had been given the one did NOTHING WITH IT. In other words, in his Christian life here and now, he did not overcome, he did not grow spiritually—he developed no character. The pounds or talents in these two parables represent the initial measure of God's Holy Spirit given at conversion. But as the Spirit-begotten person is continually *led* by the Holy Spirit— following where God's Spirit opens his understanding, *growing* in spiritual knowledge and overcoming—the measure of God's Spirit in him *increases*. But Jesus was *filled* with the Holy Spirit—not by measure (John 3:34). The parables show that the convert who does not GROW in Spirit and character development will lose out! He represents one who "RECEIVED CHRIST" and considered he was already "born again" but did not think he needed to overcome, grow spiritually, or develop spiritual character. He thought he was "already saved." He said he didn't believe in salvation by "works." What he didn't realize is that while salvation is a FREE GIFT, we are REWARDED according to our works (Matthew 16:27). But by doing NOTHING, he lost not ONLY the reward, but he lost out on the free GIFT of eternal life.

Christ's answer to such, when He returns with the KINGDOM OF GOD, is, "Thou wicked and slothful servant.... Take therefore the talent from him.... And cast ye the unprofitable servant into outer darkness: there shall be weeping and gnashing of teeth" (Matthew 25:26-30). He failed utterly in God's real PURPOSE—reproducing in us the holy, righteous CHARACTER that we may receive from God.

Many have been deceived into a FALSE "salvation."

To conclude the parallel: As the physical fetus gradually develops the *physical* features, organs and characteristics one by one, even so the begotten Christian must develop the SPIRITUAL ATTRIBUTES during this life, one by one—*love, faith, spiritual knowledge, patience, gentleness, kindness* and *temperance*. He must be a DOER of the Word of God. The fetus that fails to grow would die and never be born!

BRIDGING THE GAP

Finally, HOW has God planned to "bridge the gap" from physical to spiritual composition—to reproduce Himself out of PHYSICAL HUMANS THAT COME FROM THE PHYSICAL GROUND?

First, God put IN the physical MAN a "human" spirit. It is NOT, however, the human spirit that makes the decisions, comes to repentance, or builds the character. As I have emphasized, this spirit does not impart life, cannot see, hear, feel or think. It empowers the PHYSICAL MAN, through his BRAIN, to do these things. But this spirit RECORDS every thought—every bit of knowledge received *through* the five senses, and it records whatever character—good or bad—that is developed in human life.

The human MAN is made literally from CLAY. God is like the master potter forming and shaping a vessel out of clay. But if the clay is too hard, it will not bend into the form and shape he wants. If it is too soft and moist, it lacks firmness to "STAY PUT" where the potter bends it.

Notice in Isaiah 64:8: "But now, O [Eternal], thou art our father; we are the clay, and thou our potter; and we all are the work of thy hand."

Yet God has given each of us a MIND OF HIS OWN. If one REFUSES to acknowledge God or God's ways—refuses to repent of the wrong and turn to the right, God cannot take him and create godly character in him. But the human CLAY must be pliable, must yield willingly. If the human stiffens up and resists, he is like clay that is too dry and stiff. The potter can do nothing with it. It will not give and bend. Also, if he is so lacking in will, purpose and determination that he won't "stay put" when God molds him partly into what God wants him to be—too wishy-washy, weak, lacking root of character—he will never endure to the end. He will lose out.

We are, in truth, the WORK OF HIS HANDS. Yet WE ourselves must do our part in this spiritual development. If we lazily neglect Bible study and prayer—or if we let other material interests become more important and we NEGLECT such great salvation, we lose out.

But if we have the strength of character to YIELD, OF OUR OWN WILL to put ourselves in God's hands, HE will instill within us

His Spirit and by it His righteousness—His character—open our minds to His spiritual knowledge. We have to want it! We have to work at it! We have to put it first, above all else.

It must be God's righteousness, for all of ours is like filthy rags to Him. He continually instills His knowledge, His righteousness, His character within us—if we diligently seek it and want it. But we have our very important part in it. Then all credit goes to God.

As we receive the character of God through the Holy Spirit of God, more and more God is reproducing Himself in us.

Finally, in the resurrection, we shall be as God—in a position where we cannot sin, because we ourselves have set it so and have turned from sin and have struggled and struggled against sin and overcome sin.

God's purpose *WILL* be accomplished!

WHY MADE FROM MATERIAL SUBSTANCE?

Once again, stop and think!

Why did God choose to make man out of physical matter instead of spirit? He made angels out of spirit.

Remember God's purpose is to reproduce Himself! His divine children are to be *begotten* of Him and then born into His God Family. Christ, our Pioneer, was begotten by the Father in a manner no one else ever was, when conceived by the Holy Spirit in the virgin Mary. He was the begotten (the only begotten, in that manner) Son of God from human conception and birth. He is already the firstborn of many brethren (Romans 8:29), born a Son of God by a resurrection from the dead (Romans 1:4), as we may be later.

To show the preeminence above angels that is already Christ's and also is our potential, remember we are joint-heirs with Christ, and God says of Christ, "Being made so much better than the angels, as he hath by inheritance obtained a more excellent name than they. For unto which of the angels said he at any time, Thou art my Son, this day have I begotten thee?" (Hebrews 1:4-5). In the book of Job angels are spoken of as sons of God in chapters 1, 2 and 7, but only as created "sons." Still, as in Hebrews 1, God never said to them, "You are my own *begotten* sons." But when *we* humans receive the Holy

Spirit of God, we do become His *begotten* sons and His heirs, to receive by inheritance His NAME—just as my begotten sons inherited my name.

When we are BORN of God, we shall BE spirit. Then why did God form man in the first place of material substance—out of the earth?

I have partially answered that question already. Angels, being spirit, are immortal. Those who sinned shall go on bearing their punishment forever. Their punishment is NOT death. Their punishment is loss of the glorious opportunity God gave them to accomplish His purpose on Earth, and to live forever in the resentment, bitterness, attitude of rebellion, and utter hopelessness and frustration of mind their own sins brought upon them. Once they perverted their own minds, they can never regain balance. Happiness and joy has left them forever.

Whereas, if MAN, composed of matter, sinned and refused to repent and turn from his sin, he will die the second death—he shall utterly PERISH (John 3:16)—he will be as though he had not been (Obadiah 16). This reflects God's MERCY.

THE PHYSICAL CHANGES, THE SPIRITUAL IS CHANGELESS

But there is another all-important reason. As the humanist philosopher Elbert Hubbard said, "Nothing is permanent but change." Matter does not remain *as it is,* unchanged, permanently. But it continues *changing* permanently. Perhaps stone or iron is as unchanging as any element. But after a few thousand years, the giant stones in the wall around Jerusalem, for instance, have lost all their newness and show their age. Whatever you see now on this Earth in time will CHANGE.

Spirit, however, is CHANGELESS—except as God instilled in angel beings the power of mind—of thinking, reasoning, making decisions and exercising *will* to act on decisions or choices. But spirit substance apart from the mind power of God or spirit beings is CHANGELESS. Once Satan and his demons *made* the decision they did, being spirit, they cannot change!

In reproducing Himself God requires righteous CHARACTER DEVELOPMENT. And that requires CHANGE. If God had made us of spirit, once the decision was made to reject God, we could never have repented—could not *change* from Satan's WAY to God's! Man, composed of matter, is subject to CHANGE. Man, if called by God, can be made to realize that he has sinned, and he can REPENT—CHANGE from his sin—turn to GOD's WAY. And once his course is changed, with God's help he can pursue it. He can GROW in spiritual knowledge, develop character, overcome wrong habits, weaknesses and faults.

And this is all done by the PHYSICAL MAN, through the PHYSICAL BRAIN.

The human spirit in man empowers the brain with physical intellect, and the Spirit of God united with it empowers the brain with spiritual comprehension, and these spirits RECORD the knowledge and the character and preserve them, as well as the physical shape and appearance. These spirits do not develop the righteous character, but through the Holy Spirit God does give us His faith, His righteousness—as long as we ourselves earnestly desire it. But once holy and righteous character is developed in physical man, *HOW* does God bridge the gap, changing MAN into SPIRIT?

THE SPIRIT MOLD

I have shown you that the Scriptures picture man as the clay—which he literally is—and God as our Potter. We might call God, also, our SCULPTOR, for with our submission and eager willingness, we are the WORK OF HIS HANDS in spiritual and character development. As Job said, "If a man die, shall he live again? all the days of my appointed time will I wait, till my CHANGE come. Thou shalt call, and I will answer thee [in the resurrection]: thou wilt have a desire to *the work of thine hands*" (Job 14:14-15).

This brings us to the question of death of the physical MAN, and the resurrection—Job called it the "CHANGE"—into the Kingdom of God.

Now notice, as quoted before, in Isaiah 64:8: "But now, O [Eternal], thou art our father; we are the clay, and thou our potter; and we all are the work of thy hand."

God could not form, shape, *change,* and develop His character in us—once we had *sinned,* as all have—had we been made of spirit.

Notice further: "...Shall the clay say to him that fashioneth it, What makest thou? or thy work, He hath no hands?" (Isaiah 45:9).

Another passage of Scripture so often misapplied says: "For by grace are ye saved through faith; and that not of yourselves: it [the faith] is the gift of God: Not of works..." (Ephesians 2:8-9). We do not *earn* salvation by good works or gain it by works—BUT *when* we receive it as God's GIFT, *the degree of reward* will be according to our "works" (Matthew 16:27)—performance in living GOD's WAY—building character.

But now read the rest of this passage which is nearly always purposely omitted by those MISleading people on this point: "Not of works"...WHY?... "lest any man should boast. *For we are HIS WORKMANSHIP,* created in Christ Jesus UNTO GOOD WORKS, *which God hath before ordained that we should walk in them*" (Ephesians 2:9-10).

I have tried to point out that we must gain contact with God and that HE is the Potter—or Sculptor—fashioning, molding and shaping our lives and righteous character into His CHARACTER IMAGE, *AS WE DESIRE AND YIELD.*

All right. The godly character in us, I have stated, cannot be created by fiat. It must be developed. We must yield. We must desire it, seek it. But it comes from GOD. Thus if we keep a close daily contact with our Creator, through His Spirit and through our spirit—for remember, His Holy Spirit "beareth witness with our spirit, that we are the children of God" (Romans 8:16)—then He is fashioning and shaping our characters. Had God made us of spirit, this could not be done once we had sinned.

Now, as Job brought out, we die. Afterlife comes through the resurrection. When we die, all consciousness ceases. This is covered in Chapter 12. The physical brain becomes unconscious and decays.

With what BODY do we come, in the resurrection? That question is answered in 1 Corinthians 15: "But some man will say, How are the dead raised up? and with what body do they come?... [T]hat which thou sowest [burial in the ground], thou sowest NOT that body that shall be, but bare grain, it may chance of wheat, or of some other grain: But God giveth it a body as it hath pleased him..." (verses 35-38).

The body that dies is NOT the same body that will come up in the resurrection.

Now we come to a MOST IMPORTANT part concerning the SPIRIT IN MAN—which I have termed the "human spirit." It does not impart human life. It does not see, hear or think. The HUMAN MAN makes his decisions, and it is in the physical MAN that character must be built. It is the human CLAY that God forms into His character. The SPIRIT in man RECORDS what the brain comes to know, even the attitude, the facets of CHARACTER, not only of the human brain, but also of the whole body. It keeps the imprint even of the fingerprints.

Compare it to a sculptor's mold. The sculptor may want to produce a bronze statue of a man. The sculptor might use clay to form a clay model—or plaster of paris. Then the sculptor makes a MOLD of the model he has formed and shaped. The mold is a hollow form, made from the finished model. Into the mold is poured molten liquid bronze which then solidifies. The mold is removed, and the bronze figure is an EXACT copy of the original model.

The spirit that is in every human acts as a MOLD. It PRESERVES the human's MEMORY, his CHARACTER, his FORM AND SHAPE.

Now I do not conceive, naturally, that the spirit is a hollow form. But it supplies the same purpose as the sculptor's mold. If one has received the Holy Spirit, then in the resurrection, God will provide a SPIRIT BODY, formed and shaped by the spirit mold. The resurrected being will be COMPOSED of SPIRIT, not matter as the human model was. In the resurrected SPIRIT form he will suddenly come ALIVE. It will seem like the next flash of a second from his loss of consciousness at time of death. He will have all his memory intact. He will look as he did in human life in form and shape. Even his fingerprints will be the same.

The CHARACTER which he allowed God to build within him will be there. He will be alive FOREVER! And, like God the Father, by his own will, he will have been made so that he CANNOT sin (1 John 3:9).

The body that comes in the resurrection is not the same body that was flesh and blood in this human lifetime. God does not turn flesh and blood matter INTO spirit. The flesh-and-blood physical body, after death, decomposes and decays, but the spirit that was IN that body, like the sculptor's mold, preserves all the form and shape, the memory and the character INTACT. And that mold, being spirit, does not *change*—even though the resurrection may take place thousands of years after death.

Notice what happens AT DEATH.

"Then shall the dust return to the earth as it was: and the spirit shall return unto God who gave it" (Ecclesiastes 12:7). After death, whether buried in the earth, cremated, or what, the physical body returns to the earth. But the spirit that was IN the man, now having recorded everything—the body's form and shape, the facial identity, the memory and the character—returns to God. It will be PRESERVED *UNCHANGED*.

Such saints as Abraham, Moses, David and Daniel died thousands of years ago. STOP AND THINK ABOUT *THAT!* God had to provide some way to PRESERVE the form, shape, appearance, mind and character of saints for thousands of years. They were composed of corruptible flesh and blood. All that was THEM (man is composed wholly of matter) long since decomposed. Yet in the resurrection, it will seem to them as the next fraction of a second since loss of consciousness at death.

In the interim of death, they knew absolutely NOTHING. Says God's Word, "For the living know that they shall die: but *the dead* KNOW NOT ANY THING ..." (Ecclesiastes 9:5).

The spirit which returns to God is the human spirit that was in them throughout life. It was not an "immortal soul," for the soul was mortal and corruptible.

Those who died with God's Holy Spirit will be in the first resurrection (Revelation 20:4-5). They will come forth IMMORTAL, in a glorious body of SPIRIT composition, their faces aglow as the SUN.

All others who have not been called to eternal salvation by God during their human lifetimes will be resurrected after the thousand-year reign of the Kingdom of God under Christ, in the Great White Throne Judgment (Revelation 20:11-12). They will be resurrected MORTAL, once again in a flesh-and-blood physical body, just as before. In this great judgment they will be "called"—their eyes opened to God's truth. Then, finally, there will be a last resurrection (Revelation 20:13-15) of those who HAD been called by God in their mortal human life, but had rejected or turned from the truth. They, with those who reject it in the Great White Throne Judgment, will be in the lake of fire (2 Peter 3:10-11), which is the second death. They then shall be ashes under the soles of the feet of the immortals in God's Kingdom (Malachi 4:3), and will be as though they had never been (Obadiah 16).

Then, ahead of the millions of immortal redeemed, shall lie the tremendous awesome HUMAN POTENTIAL—when God the Creator shall have put THE ENTIRE UNIVERSE under our jurisdiction (Hebrews 2:7-8).

But there is MUCH MORE yet to be revealed. WHY all the troubles, sufferings, heartaches and evils in the world these past 6,000 years? There is of necessity a CAUSE for every EFFECT.

There is yet SO MUCH of this overview of all God's truth to be revealed!

Chapter 8
Why Today's World Evils?

IT'S TIME, NOW, TO STOP A MOMENT AND GET OUR BEARINGS. We live in a world whose number-one problem is threat of HUMAN EXTINCTION! A world gripped in the clutch of immorality, crime and violence. A world fraught with suffering both physical and mental, a frustrated world staring at only hopelessness ahead!

But WHY? What has gone wrong with government, with religion, with higher education?—and WHY are more than half the world's people illiterate, poverty-stricken—many actually starving—living in filth and squalor?

Yes, WHY?

I mentioned earlier the confusion and inability to understand what one sees in a motion picture when he begins viewing at a point more than halfway through.

If one's approach to understanding today's chaotic world starts from the vantage point of what we see today, he is, indeed, confused, bewildered!

We must view the motion picture of REALITY from the beginning. That's why we have started this revelation of TRUTH at its farthermost prehistoric beginning.

We have covered the actual beginning of all things, before the material universe was, with only the two SUPREME SPIRIT PERSONAGES—one called "the Word," who was with God. The Personage called "the Word" created all things, under direction of GOD!

Their first feat of creation was the angels—individually created spirit beings—apparently many millions in number. All these were existing in physically empty space.

Then came the creation of our planet Earth and the entire physical UNIVERSE—created, apparently, simultaneously.

The Earth was populated by a third of all the angels! They were assigned to utilize the physical properties of Earth—to *produce* from the Earth—to enhance its beauty. In other words, to improve and *finish*, as it were, Earth's creation.

And now, a vital NEW TRUTH!

What God had created was perfect in quality—but, like unfinished raw furniture, the Earth's creation was to be completed by the angels. Thus the angels were to participate in acts of creation!

Actually this Earth was the *proving ground*—even as God endowed it to be for man today—to qualify the angels to perform the same creative finishing of the planets of the entire endless universe! And that has *now* become the transcendent potential of MAN!

It was imperative that the angels *work together*, in peaceful and harmonious unison. For this purpose God placed over them HIS GOVERNMENT—based on the spiritual law of God. That law is *a way of life*—the way of LOVE—of outgoing love to God and concern for the welfare of others. It is the way of GIVING—of helping, serving, sharing—of kindness, consideration and mercy.

On the throne of God's government God had placed the supreme masterpiece of His creation—the super-archangel Lucifer. This Lucifer, even as his angels, was endowed with an independent MIND—to think, reason, make choices and decisions. God's intention was to create within Lucifer and the angels, *upon their decision*, God's own holy and righteous character.

But Lucifer led his angels into rebellion. Instead of God's way of LOVE—of GIVING—they had turned to GETTING—to vanity, sin, corruption, perversion of mind! From creation to destruction.

Now to another point of NEW TRUTH! Haven't you wondered WHY Satan is still here, now subtilely swaying mankind into his ways of GETTING, seeking false values, and perversion of mind?

Think on this! Think of it as GOD viewed it! I have previously explained how ONLY GOD, of all living beings, possessed this holy and righteous character—only GOD could be positively relied on *never* to depart from His way of LOVE.

But God also knew *there were not enough* of Him! He wanted millions—even billions—of personages endowed with His holy and righteous character!

That is why God had purposed to REPRODUCE HIMSELF, through MAN!

So, (Psalm 104:30) God in six days RENEWED THE FACE OF THE EARTH—restoring it from the wasteness and decay caused by sinning angels—preparing it to become *the proving ground* of MAN to develop in man God's righteous character, and prepare him for the same transcendent potential that had been that of the angels!

Genesis 1, we have seen, records the six days of renewing the face of the Earth, preparing it for MAN.

Come now to Genesis 1:25-26: "And God made the beast of the earth after his kind, and cattle after their kind, and every thing that creepeth upon the earth after his kind: and God saw that it was good. And God said, Let us [not me] make man in our image, after our likeness [form and shape] ...." In other words, AFTER THE GOD KIND! For a very special relationship with God!

But "God formed man of the dust of the ground ..." (Genesis 2:7)—not out of spirit as angels had been formed.

Now CONSIDER CAREFULLY!

The first man, Adam, was given the opportunity to QUALIFY to replace the former Lucifer on the THRONE OF THE GOVERNMENT OF GOD.

But—note carefully this!—to qualify, Adam had to not only accept God's GOVERNMENT and way of life—it was imperative that he also HAD TO REJECT AND TURN FROM the way of Satan.

He had to OVERCOME Satan and his way!

Let me remind the reader at this point that the first 11 chapters of Genesis are an exceedingly BRIEF synopsis of events of the first more than 2,000 years of human life on Earth—up to the time of Abraham. Details must be filled in either by what is obviously implied, or by records found elsewhere in the Bible.

God fully explained to Adam and Eve His GOVERNMENT—His spiritual LAW and way of life—and that, upon Adam's right

CHOICE, he could qualify, receive the Holy Spirit of God, begetting him as a SON OF GOD. Also God explained to Adam and Eve the CONSEQUENCES of rejection and disobedience:

This was symbolized by the tree of the knowledge of good and evil. For, warned God, "in the day that thou eatest thereof, THOU SHALT SURELY DIE" (Genesis 2:17).

Then God allowed Adam and Eve to be tested by Satan. But Satan was subtile. He got to Adam through his wife, Eve. Eve was deceived—but Adam was not.

Eve "took of the fruit" of the forbidden tree, "and did eat, and gave also unto her husband with her; and he did eat" (Genesis 3:6).

So, "[N]ow," said God, "*lest* he put forth his hand, and take also of the tree of life, and eat, and live for ever; Therefore the [Eternal] God sent him forth from the garden of Eden, to till the ground from whence he was taken. So he drove out the man; and he placed at the east of the garden of Eden Cherubims, and a flaming sword which turned every way, to keep the way of the tree of life"—LEST he and his children go back and take of the tree symbolizing God's Holy Spirit (verses 22-24).

In other words, when Adam deliberately took of the forbidden tree, to put it in modern language, Adam said to God, "God, my Maker, I reject you as my God, I REJECT your way of life. I REJECT your GOVERNMENT over me. I elect to continue in the way I choose; I want you to keep your nose out of my affairs. I reject you as the source of basic knowledge—I have taken to myself the determination of the knowledge of what is right and what is wrong."

And God replied, "I have set clearly before you the way of truth. YOU HAVE DECIDED—therefore I SENTENCE YOU and the world that shall come from you to 6,000 years of being CUT OFF FROM ME. GO, form your own governments. Form your own religions. Produce your own knowledge, cut off from revealed truth, and devise your own system of disseminating such false knowledge. Live according to your own distorted sense of values. But, during this 6,000 years I shall call into my service such as I shall choose, for the fulfillment of MY PURPOSE."

Now WHY was it necessary to leave Satan on Earth, free to sway and deceive all mankind for 6,000 years? There were TWO reasons:

1) Those God called to His service and to salvation during this 6,000 years were required, as had been Adam, to QUALIFY to reign in the GOVERNMENT OF GOD. And how? By rejecting and overcoming Satan and his way—as well as by voluntarily choosing GOD'S WAY!

2) God's GOVERNMENT requires that the throne never be vacated. The former Lucifer must remain until a successor both qualifies and also is inducted into the office.

And we might add a third reason. God ordained that 6,000 years of sinning human existence PROVE, for ALL TIME, that Satan's way can result only in evils, suffering, frustration, hopelessness and death. God is allowing Satan to deceive and sway mankind for 6,000 years to PROVE this truth, not only to the human race, but to the other two thirds of the angels.

During this 6,000 years there have been three epochs, as differentiated from the two worlds of the antediluvian world culminating with the Noachian Flood, and this present evil world, which shall culminate with Christ's coming to usher in the WORLD TOMORROW.

These three epochs are 1) all the time from the Adamic creation of MAN to the Old Covenant made at Mount Sinai with Israel; 2) the epoch of the "Old Testament Church" (congregation of Israel); 3) the Church of God of the New Testament. These will be discussed in Chapter 9.

But it should be clear, at this point, what is the CAUSE of today's world evils. The presence of Satan, and his invisible, subtile, yet superpowerful sway (see Chapter 11 on human nature) over mankind is the basic CAUSE. The WAY OF LIFE Satan has injected into human minds—the way of vanity, lust and greed—of jealousy and envy—of competition and strife—of rebellion and deceit—these things we generally term "human nature" are the direct and specific *cause*. And all humanity has suffered the *effect!*

Remember though, God had made an exception. He purposed to call those few HE would choose to do what He required.

Some 1,900 years went by. Apparently Adam's second son, Abel, had been called, for Christ called him "righteous Abel" (Matthew 23:35). Enoch "walked with God." Then God called Noah. He was perfect in his physical descent, or generations, and also walked with God. God called him in order to save humans alive during the Flood.

God called Abraham to forsake the life of Babylon—to come out, as it were, from Satan's civilization—and turn to God's way. Abraham had not sought God—yet he was a rare exception, in that he obeyed without question or excuse.

Four hundred and thirty years after Abraham, God called Moses. Moses had been prepared for his calling, having been reared as a prince in the palace of Pharaoh. But Moses, humanly, protested. He had never sought God or the commission to which God called him. He protested, saying in effect, "Oh I can't do it, Lord. I have an impediment of speech—I stutter." So then God told Moses He had appointed his brother Aaron to be his spokesman.

God said to Moses, in effect, "You *WILL* do what I command you!" And thereupon, he did.

God had called Moses to lead the descendants of Abraham—by then numbering some 2 or 3 million—out of Egyptian slavery. To these "children of Israel" at Mount Sinai God made a proposition: If they would become HIS NATION, governed by His laws and statutes, He would make them the head-most nation on Earth—with the tremendous national and temporal blessings (this life only) of becoming the most prosperous, most powerful, most peaceful nation on Earth. The people agreed.

Thereupon God entered into a COVENANT with them—later called "the Old Covenant," mediated by Moses. It was a marriage agreement, by which Israel agreed to obey her Husband (God), and God agreed to make them, on obedience, Earth's number-one nation. But Satan was still on Earth, and busy. The Israelites turned to spiritual adultery, worse than a human harlot.

God called Jonah for a special mission to warn the city of Nineveh of impending destruction. Jonah tried to run away from God on a ship. But when God calls one for a special mission, God sees to it that the mission is performed!

God called the Prophet Isaiah. He protested he was a man of unclean lips. But God cleansed his lips. Then Isaiah answered, "Here I am. Send me."

God called the Prophet Jeremiah. Indeed he was, like Jesus later, sanctified before he was born. Yet he held up his hands and protested, "But I am too young." God said sternly, "Thou *shalt* go to all that I shall send thee." Jeremiah went!

The Apostle Paul, originally named Saul, burned up energy and zeal persecuting the Church of God. But God struck him down, brought him to his senses, and he then became one of the greatest of the men of God since Adam.

I, myself, certainly did not choose God. I chose the profession of advertising and journalism. When I was 25, an angel, in an intensive dream to my wife of a few days, revealed that God was calling me to His service. I was merely embarrassed. Becoming a minister of Jesus Christ was the *last* thing I should have wanted to do.

"I don't know whether that dream had any meaning," I said. "Why not tell it to the minister of the church on the corner—maybe he can tell you whether it means anything." As Jonah, Paul and others had been allowed to go their own way for a while, this unusual dream was soon forgotten—for the time. One decade went by. Then God stirred me to the most intensive, almost day-and-night, study and research of my life, resulting from dual challenges that struck at my vanity.

This intensive Bible study resulted in sweeping my mind clean of all previous religious assumptions, then opening my mind to the UNDERSTANDING of God's Word—bringing me to a *real* repentance—being CONQUERED by God and His Word in unconditional surrender—and, in living FAITH, turning over to HIM a life I felt was worthless. I humbly gave it to Him, if He could use it. And, like others He has conquered before me, He has used it these 51 years!

Back, now, to the thread of our story. In His due time, God sent forth His only begotten Son—the former "Word" who had been eternally with God.

He was the "second Adam."

Like the first Adam, He had not only to BELIEVE and OBEY God—but also to reject and overcome Satan and his way!

Oh yes! He was TEMPTED in all points like the rest of us sinning mortals—only HE NEVER SINNED!

Satan was still around. He was vehemently *aroused* at the appearing of this second Adam. Jesus was the Messenger of the NEW Covenant, bearing the message of that covenant from God. That message was HIS GOSPEL! Satan was determined to prevent that message from being proclaimed! For it included the abolition of Satan from Earth!

He tried to have the Christ-child killed as an infant. But God saved His Son Jesus! For some 30 years, Jesus had faced temptations from Satan, but had safely overcome!

Then came the most severe temptation ever thrown at any man. Jesus had fasted 40 days and 40 nights without a morsel of food or a drop of water. But this fasting brought Him even closer to God His Father. Though physically weak, He was spiritually STRONG. The story of that temptation is revealed in the first 11 verses of Matthew 4.

It was the most titanic contest ever fought. Jesus was tempted as no man had ever been. Yet He resisted and overcame Satan, and remained faithful to GOD's way!

Satan's very effort to overthrow Jesus resulted in Jesus's qualification to replace him and restore the GOVERNMENT OF GOD. More, to establish the KINGDOM OF GOD, which is the FAMILY OF GOD, ruling with the GOVERNMENT OF GOD!

Jesus had been required to OVERCOME SATAN—to resist and defeat him—in order to QUALIFY to sit on the THRONE OF THE WHOLE EARTH!

But what about those God *has called,* from Abel until now?

Notice something that seems to have escaped all churches, theological seminaries, and students of the Bible.

Notice what Christ Himself said, in Revelation 3:21: "To him that overcometh will I grant to sit with me in my throne, even as I also overcame, and am set down with my Father in his throne."

To him that *overcomes*—overcomes WHAT? Notice, overcomes *"even as* I also overcame." What was Jesus required *to overcome,* to qualify to sit, first, now, on His Father's throne, and, next, on *His own throne*—the throne of David, in Jerusalem?

CONSIDER! *Think* on this! If Jesus was required to overcome Satan—the former Lucifer—who is still on the throne where God originally placed him—in order to QUALIFY to succeed the disqualified Lucifer on that throne—should we humans be required to do less, in that we ALSO may sit on that throne with Christ?

Mark well this fact! What Jesus is quoted above as saying applies ONLY to those called *BEFORE* Christ's return in ALL

POWER AND GLORY—to sit with Him *when* He sits on that throne!

I have said repeatedly, THE WORLD AS A WHOLE IS CUT OFF from all contact with God—for 6,000 years dating from Adam! Jesus said plainly, "*No man can* come to me, except the Father which hath sent me draw him..." (John 6:44). Unless CALLED—drawn—by God the Father, ALL HUMANITY IS TOTALLY CUT OFF FROM GOD!

What, then? Is there injustice with God? Are all others LOST?—condemned without a chance to the ultimate second death in "the lake of fire"?

Positively *NO!*

I will show you that those NOT CALLED are simply NOT JUDGED. They are NOT "lost"—neither are they "saved." What a tragedy that those professing Christianity have been themselves CUT OFF from this TRUTH!

But first, notice what Jesus also said, recorded in Revelation 2:26-27: "And he that overcometh, and keepeth my works unto the end, to him will I give power over the nations: And he shall rule them with a rod of iron...."

Those called and drawn by God must keep on overcoming Satan *"unto the end"* of this life! But they not only then shall sit with Christ in His throne—they shall, under Him, RULE over all nations. This shall be the fulfillment of Daniel's prophecy of 7:18.

GOD'S FESTIVALS PORTRAY THE MASTER PLAN BEING WORKED OUT HERE BELOW

We now come to an eye-opening revelation, indeed!

God gave His annual festivals, with their seven annual holy days (sabbaths), to His "Church"—then called the congregation of Israel—in the days of Moses!

They were intended to picture to the people of God, repeatedly every year, His master plan of redemption—leading to the incredible HUMAN POTENTIAL!

These festivals were ordained to be kept FOREVER! Jesus, the apostles, and the early Church of God, ALL OBSERVED THEM! But, so far as the author knows, only one Church continues to observe them today—the Church of God!

They reveal a startling TRUTH, otherwise obscured from human knowledge!

The human race began with Adam. But spiritual salvation and qualification for the transcendent HUMAN POTENTIAL begins with CHRIST. The physical human creation began with Adam—but the SPIRITUAL CREATION begins with the second Adam!

It BEGINS with the forgiveness of sin—following *real* repentance—being *conquered* by God—and the living FAITH that *believes* what Christ says!

Therefore the *first* of these festivals was the PASSOVER. It pictures to God's people annually the shed blood of Christ—the "Lamb of God" sacrificed to pay the PENALTY of sin we humans have brought on ourselves, in our stead.

Then followed the festival of UNLEAVENED BREAD—seven days in which no leaven may be eaten, or found in the houses of God's people. Leaven puffs up—as does VANITY, the epitome of sin. This festival lasts seven days, immediately following the Passover—with the first and last of the seven being annual holy days (holy convocations).

These first festivals come in the spring—the 14th through the 21st days of the first month of God's SACRED year. They, with the feast of FIRSTFRUITS (PENTECOST in the New Testament), fall in the spring—representing, as at Jerusalem, the FIRST, or early, GRAIN HARVEST. The feast of firstfruits (Pentecost) reminds God's people every year that they, prior to Christ's Second Coming, are merely the comparatively very small FIRST spiritual harvest—while all but the few God has called are CUT OFF from God and His spiritual salvation.

The remaining four festivals come during the autumnal harvest time—picturing the MAIN spiritual harvest. These occur at the time of the main harvest of foodstuffs, in the fall of the year.

The fourth festival, a single holy day, is the Feast of TRUMPETS. It pictures the coming of Christ in supreme POWER and GLORY to rule all nations—and to open spiritual salvation to ALL THEN LIVING!

The fifth annual festival is another single holy day—a FAST day. It is called, in the Bible, the DAY OF ATONEMENT. It is observed by Judaism as "Yom Kippur." This most solemn day pictures Christ's banishment of Satan, that humanity at last may be made "AT ONE" with God. Therefore it is called the day of AT-ONE-MENT, or "Atonement." A humanity CUT OFF from God cannot be AT ONE with Him—until Satan is removed, and ALL shall be called and drawn by God—IF they will—to spiritual salvation through Christ.

Five days later follows the festival of TABERNACLES for seven days. This festival pictures the PRINCIPLE spiritual harvest—during the thousand years that Christ and those who have qualified shall rule all nations. Satan will be banished—into the biblically symbolic "bottomless pit." Overcoming Satan naturally will no longer be a requirement. The first of these seven days is an annual sabbath.

Then, the next day following the Feast of Tabernacles is a one-day festival—also the seventh annual sabbath.

It pictures a resurrection to judgment of all previously uncalled by God—all who ever lived—billions who lived under Satan's way and died uncalled—neither then "lost" or "saved" spiritually. These billions will be resurrected MORTAL—as they were—flesh-and-blood humans. *Then* they shall look back on the 6,000 years of Satan's sway—of human wrongdoing, sin, and consequent suffering, anguish and death. Then, for their first time, God shall call them. Satan will be banished forever! But they still shall have to make their own DECISIONS!

With the 6,000-year record of world evils swayed by Satan, and the 1,000-year record of humanity taught by Christ and immortal saints, they may look at the record—and compare.

We may HOPE that virtually all, if not all, will yield themselves to God's call, and receive spiritual salvation and ETERNAL LIFE!

But that is not yet all!

There then (Revelation 20:13) shall follow a final resurrection of those who *had* been called to spiritual redemption during all 7,000 years, and who had rejected God's loving mercy, and rebelled, KNOWING the truth! They will then be required to REALIZE FULLY what they have rejected and rebelled against. They shall all have died once—and now they shall die the second and final, eternal DEATH, in the lake of fire—described in 2 Peter 3:7, 10.

But their days of suffering shall be over as revealed in Malachi 4:1-3. They shall be left neither root nor branch—they shall be ashes under the soles of the feet of those living. They shall be as though they had not been (Obadiah 16-17).

But of the saved immortals, "... there shall be no more death, neither sorrow, nor crying, neither shall there be any more pain: for the former things are passed away" (Revelation 21:4).

Chapter 9
Why the Church?

ONE CANNOT COMPREHEND THE REAL PURPOSE AND FUNCTION of the Church without an understanding of Old Testament ISRAEL.

Ancient Israel was both church and state. It was one of the world's nations, called the kingdom of Israel. But it also was a church, called the congregation of Israel. Or, as in Acts 7:38, the "church in the wilderness."

One cannot understand either Old Testament Israel or the New Testament Church of God unless he bears in mind God's PURPOSE in placing mankind on the Earth.

God is reproducing Himself! His cardinal objective for MAN is the creation of holy, righteous, spiritual CHARACTER. Bear that constantly in mind as we compare, or contrast, the Old Testament "church in the wilderness" and the New Testament Church of God. Creation of this righteous character prepares for the *ultimate objective*.

We have explained the natural mind of man—and how it differs from animal brain. There is, in man, a spirit. This spirit is in the form of essence—not a soul or person. It imparts to the human brain the power of intellect—of thinking, reasoning, decision making. This is explained in detail in Chapter 7.

This mind, then, with which each human is born is the natural, carnal human mind. And "the carnal mind is enmity [hostile] against God: for it is not subject to the law of God, neither indeed can be" (Romans 8:7). This mind is *limited* to the acquisition of physical knowledge.

To comprehend the things of God—spiritual knowledge—is impossible without receiving as God's gift His Holy Spirit—a second spirit added to the "human" spirit with which each person is born.

God's creation of MAN was perfect *as a physical creation,* yet incomplete! This physical creation began with Adam, but the spiritual creation must begin with the second Adam—Jesus Christ.

When God sentenced Adam's human race to 6,000 years of being CUT OFF from contact with God, He made an exception. He reserved to Himself the prerogative of calling into His service such as He required to fulfill His PURPOSE!

God had called Abraham. And 430 years after, God called Abraham's descendants through Isaac and Israel, then called "the children of Israel." At that time they were in Egyptian slavery. Under leadership of Moses, God led them out of Egypt, to inherit the Promised Land.

At Mount Sinai, God offered them a covenant agreement, later called "the Old Covenant." Upon obedience to GOD'S GOVERNMENT over them, God promised to make them the most prosperous, most powerful nation on Earth. But God promised them *only* temporal, material and national rewards—NOT His Holy Spirit of eternal life.

This hostile mind, unsubmissive to God, we shall see in Chapter 10, had been subtilely and invisibly injected into human minds through the human spirit, by Satan. A baby is not born with it. The "prince of the power of the air" (Ephesians 2:2) begins implanting it as early in life as the human mind begins to absorb knowledge and to function.

Modern intellectuals have said, "Given sufficient KNOWLEDGE, the human mind can solve all problems."

One of God's purposes in Old Covenant Israel was to PROVE, by multiple generations of Israelites, that, even given KNOWLEDGE of God's government and way of life, the carnal mind will not—and therefore cannot—solve its problems, live in peace, happiness, joy, and eternal salvation.

However, humans *will not* obey God's WAY to peace, happiness, and eternal joy without the addition of *a second* spirit to the "human" spirit.

The experience of multiple generations of Israelites PROVED that the natural mind of man *is* hostile to God—not subject to the law of God, which is THE WAY to peace, happiness and abundance.

Adam and Eve had been instructed by God in HIS WAY. They rejected it, and turned to the WAY of SELF-centeredness—of vanity, lust and greed—of jealousy and envy—of competition, strife, violence and destruction.

But in Old Covenant Israel, God REVEALED to them, through Moses and the prophets, the KNOWLEDGE of God's WAY.

WHY, then, Old Covenant Israel?

They were left without excuse. They were, in Adam, a physical creation—but without the SPIRITUAL creation, which can come only through Christ the "second Adam," they simply *would not* live the way of life that produces peace and universal well-being.

I repeat, they were without excuse! It was MAN—the first Adam—who thought he could live a more happy life, without God's Spirit, which he spurned.

God sent to Old Covenant Israelites His prophets, bearing His admonitions, PLEADING with them. They stoned many of their prophets to death!

Through the Prophet Jeremiah, God pleaded: "Return, thou backsliding Israel, saith the [Eternal]; and I will not cause mine anger to fall upon you: for I am merciful, saith the [Eternal] .... Only acknowledge thine iniquity, that thou hast transgressed against the [Eternal] thy God, and hast scattered thy ways to the strangers [Gentile nations] under every green tree, and ye have not obeyed my voice, saith the [Eternal]."

"Turn," God continued, "O backsliding children, saith the [Eternal]; for I am married unto you ..." (Jeremiah 3:12-14).

Old Covenant Israel was carnal-minded, with minds hostile against God, and not subject to the laws and ways of God!

NOW THE NEW TESTAMENT CHURCH OF GOD

Remember Old Covenant Israel lived in the days of the first Adam. Satan, the "prince of the power of the air," by subtile injection through the "human" spirit of his hostile attitude, ruled supreme in the world. And with the exception of those in God's Church, he does still today!

Remember, too, that all nations and peoples, except the nation Israel, had been completely CUT OFF from God and knowledge of God. They had continued forming their own ideas of government, swayed, though unrealized, by Satan. They had formed their own religions—created in their own imaginations their own gods. They had produced their own store of human materialistic knowledge—though more than half of all living were—and remain today—illiterate, living in abject poverty, filth and squalor. They were suffering the evil consequences of Satan's way!

It was, and today still is, except for the Church of God and the message of HOPE it disseminates, A WORLD WITHOUT HOPE!

But Jesus Christ, the second Adam, was to come at God's proper time, bringing a hope that is real—and transcendently wonderful beyond human capacity to comprehend!

Notice two prophecies, recorded by Old Testament prophets under inspiration of God:

"For unto us [the Israelitish people] a child is born, unto us a son is given: and the GOVERNMENT shall be upon his shoulder: and his name shall be called Wonderful, Counsellor, The mighty God, The everlasting Father, The Prince of Peace. Of the increase of his GOVERNMENT and peace there shall be no end, upon the throne of David, and upon his kingdom, to order it, and to establish it with judgment and with justice from henceforth even for ever. The zeal of the [Eternal] of hosts will perform this" (Isaiah 9:6-7).

This prophecy foretells Christ's appearing as a KING—a RULER—to reestablish the GOVERNMENT OF GOD on Earth.

Then, foretelling His coming as the Savior of mankind, "Therefore the Lord himself shall give you a sign; Behold, a virgin shall conceive, and bear a son, and shall call his name Immanuel" (Isaiah 7:14).

Now see this prophecy fulfilled in the New Testament: An angel appeared to Joseph, fiancé of Mary the mother of Jesus:

"Joseph," he said, "thou son of David, fear not to take unto thee Mary thy [espoused] wife: for that which is conceived in her is of the Holy [Spirit]. And she shall bring forth a son, and thou shalt call his name JESUS: for he shall save his people from their sins. Now all this was done, that it might be fulfilled which was spoken of the Lord by the prophet, saying, Behold, a virgin shall be with child, and shall bring forth a son, and they shall call his name Emmanuel, which being interpreted is, God with us" (Matthew 1:20-23).

This prophecy reveals Christ as SAVIOR.

And so was born JESUS—the SECOND ADAM! Begotten of God before His human birth—as no other had been. He was GOD as well as man—GOD with us—GOD made human so that, as a human, He could die (Hebrews 2:9) for humans! Yes, GOD in the likeness of human flesh, who could overcome Satan the former King Lucifer, thus qualifying to restore the GOVERNMENT OF GOD to Earth!

Satan tried to destroy Jesus soon after birth—before He could grow up to qualify and announce the KINGDOM OF GOD! But God protected the Christ-child, causing Joseph and Mary to flee with Him to Egypt—until Herod, provincial Roman king over Judea, was dead.

"And the child grew, and waxed strong in spirit, filled with wisdom..." (Luke 2:40). Jesus was endowed with the Holy Spirit of God *from birth.*

I have said that, as the "prince of the power of the air," Satan subtilely and invisibly injects into human minds through the "human" spirit his attitude of hostile rebellion. Satan begins implanting this carnal attitude as early in life as the child begins to absorb knowledge and to think. But the growing child Jesus, filled with GOD's Spirit, resisted from infancy this magnetic "pull" we call human nature.

Jesus never had a carnal mind, hostile against God. His mind, from earliest childhood, *was* subject to the law of God. Thus He was constantly and continually overcoming Satan, *in a manner no other human had experienced!*

Then, turning again to Mark's record, "And it came to pass in those days, that Jesus came from Nazareth of Galilee, and was baptized of John in Jordan. And straightway coming up out of the water, he saw the heavens opened, and the Spirit like a dove descending upon him: And there came a voice from heaven, saying, Thou art my beloved Son, in whom I am well pleased.

"And immediately the Spirit driveth him into the wilderness. And he was there in the wilderness forty days, tempted of Satan…" (Mark 1:9-13).

After 40 days and 40 nights without a morsel of food or a drop of water, Jesus was physically very weak but spiritually strong. Then ensued the most *titanic battle* ever fought—for the highest stakes of all time in the universe!

The detailed story of this supreme struggle is recorded in Matthew 4, beginning verse 1.

Many a doctor of medicine would believe no man could live 40 days without food or water. They are woefully ignorant about fasting. Jesus was, truly, somewhat close to actual starvation. Words could not describe the desperate HUNGER that gripped Him.

Satan struck directly at Jesus's weakest state at the moment. He hurled his first blow in this contest for the greatest stakes ever fought for, at what he well knew to be humanity's weakest point *both spiritually and physically*—vanity, and hunger:

"IF," Satan must have sneered insultingly, "IF thou be the Son of God, command that these stones be made bread" (verse 3).

A spiritually weaker human would have bristled up, angrily answering back, "IF I be the Son of God—*what do you mean, IF?* I'll show you whether I'm the Son of God! I'll show you I can perform miracles!" And, to satisfy His desperate hunger, He would have fallen into Satan's subtle trap!

But Jesus held fast His OBEDIENCE to GOD! He answered, "It is written," going immediately to God's Scripture, "Man shall not live by bread alone, but by every word that proceedeth out of the mouth of God"! (verse 4).

Satan had lost out on his most masterful thrust of temptation. But Satan does not give up easily! How well I know that, by experience! He struck again.

"*If* thou be the Son of God"—Satan repeated his stab at humanity's weakest point—vanity—but now under different circumstances. He had taken Jesus up to a pinnacle of the temple. "[C]ast thyself down: for it is written"—now Satan could quote Scripture, too, only he misapplied its intended meaning—"it is written, He shall give his angels charge concerning thee: and in their hands they shall bear thee up, lest at any time thou dash thy foot against a stone"—or lest inertia wallop you as gravity pulls you speedily to Earth.

He was testing Jesus's FAITH in God, as well as a repeated challenge against human vanity. Satan's ministers can quote Scripture—but they twist and distort it out of its intended contextual meaning.

Jesus came right back at Satan.

"It is written again," He said, "Thou shalt not tempt the [Eternal] thy God" (verse 7).

The scripture about angels bearing one up IF he falls applies only to an accidental fall. To jump off deliberately would be "tempting God." In other words, doubting the Word of God in its intended meaning, and TESTING God—putting God to the test, implying doubt that He would do it!

Satan had one more "ace-in-the-hole." He now tempted Jesus on lust and greed—on GETTING—on seizure of POWER!

Satan now took Jesus to the top of a high mountain, and showed Jesus all the kingdoms of this world. Then he said, "All these things will I give thee, if thou wilt fall down and worship me" (verse 9).

In other words, both Satan and Jesus knew that if Jesus QUALIFIED, He would be given RULE over the governments of all nations on Earth. But they both knew of God's 6,000-year sentence on humanity—and Jesus would have to wait almost 2,000 more years for the POWER and GLORY of world rule.

Jesus did not deny this power of rule, by Satan's subtle DECEPTIONS, was in Satan's hands. But He also knew Satan was a liar—would not keep his word—and if he did, Jesus still would have world rule only UNDER SATAN. He knew it was GOD's to give, and He was definitely prepared to wait until GOD's TIME—after the 6,000-year sentence on man, when GOD would crown Him and send Him again to Earth in supreme splendor, power and glory!

This time, Jesus decided to put an end to this colossal struggle for world power. "Get thee hence, Satan"! Jesus snapped out the command with AUTHORITY! And Satan, defeated in his bid to retain world sway, slunk away (verses 10-11).

But don't think Satan gave up! Not yet! He tried to overthrow God's apostles, and His Church. He schemed to manipulate human powers to persecute God's Church, and to SUPPRESS Christ's gospel message of WORLD HOPE! He is still warring savagely against God's Church and apostle, even in this final generation of his evil world!

But Jesus Christ lives! God is on His throne, with Jesus there at His right hand. And Satan can do only what God allows!

Back, now, to Mark 1:14-15: "Now after that John was put in prison, Jesus came into Galilee, preaching THE GOSPEL OF THE KINGDOM OF GOD, And saying, The time is fulfilled, and the KINGDOM OF GOD is at hand: repent ye, and believe the gospel." That is, believe the MESSAGE Jesus proclaimed announcing the coming world-ruling KINGDOM OF GOD!

The time was fulfilled. Jesus had QUALIFIED, where the first Adam failed, to wrest world rule from Satan—to RESTORE God's government to the Earth—to establish the Spirit-born Family of God, ruling in THE KINGDOM OF GOD!

Leaving Nazareth, Jesus took up residence in Capernaum, on the north shore of the Sea of Galilee. Jesus was no vagabond. He occupied an established home, contrary to much false supposition today.

And immediately Jesus called His disciples to Him—to teach and train them to become His apostles to go forth with His message of THE KINGDOM OF GOD, after Jesus's personal mission on Earth had ended.

Jesus was walking along the shore of the Sea of Galilee. He called to follow Him two brothers, Peter and Andrew. These brothers had not sought out Jesus. They had not aspired to become His apostles—they had chosen to be fishermen. But they now, at Jesus's word, FORSOOK ALL, and followed Him!

Next Jesus called to His discipleship two other brothers—James and John. They too, had elected to be fishermen—not apostles (Matthew 4:18-22).

Matthew had chosen to be a tax collector. But to His 12, Jesus later said, "Ye have not chosen me, but I have chosen you."

And, as in Mark 1:14-15, so in Matthew's account, "...Jesus went about all Galilee, teaching in their synagogues, and preaching the GOSPEL OF THE KINGDOM..." (Matthew 4:23).

Until Jesus had QUALIFIED to restore God's government by overcoming Satan, there could be no assurance, save in the mind and purpose of God, of the restoration of the government Satan had rejected.

For some 3½ years Jesus went about the land of Israel, preaching in their synagogues the GOOD NEWS of the world's future HOPE, teaching and training His disciples to become apostles.

Finally, after being beaten with stripes, that His Church might have physical healing, Jesus was crucified—that by His shed blood our sins might be forgiven—because He had paid *our* penalty, death, in our stead.

THE CHURCH IS BORN

After being three days and three nights dead in the tomb, Jesus was resurrected. By this resurrection, He became the *first BORN Son of God* (Romans 1:4). He was now VERY GOD Himself—the first so BORN of many brethren to follow by a later resurrection.

After His resurrection, Jesus was 40 days with His apostles, "speaking of the things pertaining to THE KINGDOM OF GOD" (Acts 1:3).

Then He ascended to heaven, to the right hand of God on the heavenly throne (Hebrews 12:2; Revelation 3:21).

Ten days later (the year was A.D. 31), came the annual holy day called "the feast of the firstfruits," and, in the New Testament, "the day of Pentecost."

Of the many thousands who had heard Jesus's proclaiming the KINGDOM OF GOD, there were, after the 3½ years, *only 120* who *believed!* (Acts 1:15).

On that festive holy day, beside the 120 disciples, there were gathered devout Jews from many parts of the world.

Then an unprecedented and amazing spectacle happened. It was the welcoming display of the coming of God's HOLY SPIRIT to fill His Church! And it has never been repeated!

It happened suddenly! "[T]here came a sound from heaven as of a rushing mighty wind, and it filled all the house where they [the 120 disciples] were sitting" (Acts 2:2). Wind can make a considerable noise. God's Holy Spirit is compared, elsewhere, to wind (John 3:8). Let it be noted that no such wind-sound is heard in modern-day "pentecostal" meetings!

But the disciples not only *heard*—they *saw* this supernatural display. "And there appeared unto them cloven tongues like as of fire, and it sat upon each of them"—each of the 120 (Acts 2:3). And they, the 120, "were all filled with the Holy

[Spirit], and began to speak with other tongues, as the Spirit gave them utterance" (verse 4).

Word of this supernatural display spread rapidly, and then it was that the many devout Jews from the many nations came running in—"and were confounded, because that every man heard them [the 120] speak in his own language" (verse 6). Note it! Each individual, in his own native language, heard *them*— the 120—speaking in his own foreign language. And they *understood* clearly, in their own various languages, what the 120 were saying. The miracle was in the HEARING, rather than the speaking!

Then Peter, chief apostle, for the first time inspired with God's Holy Spirit, preached a heart-stirring sermon, showing that Jesus was *both* Lord (King—Ruler) and Christ (Savior).

That same day God "ADDED unto them about three thousand souls" who were baptized that same day (verse 41).

And thus THE CHURCH OF GOD—the *same* Church that is known today as the WORLDWIDE CHURCH OF GOD—was born. *The line of succession* will be shown later by which the Worldwide Church of God is positively identified as the continuation of THE SAME CHURCH. [For more information on what happened to the Worldwide Church of God after Mr. Armstrong died, write for a copy of *Malachi's Message*.]

NOW WHY THE CHURCH? ITS PURPOSE

When Jesus Christ returns to Earth in supernatural splendor, power and glory, He is coming to His TEMPLE. But *where* is that temple—when will it be built?

Many students of the Bible have wondered—speculated. Will the Israelis, after all, destroy the "Dome of the Rock"—the Moslem temple standing today on the site of both Solomon's temple, and the temple to which Jesus came at His first appearing?

Malachi's prophecy says: "Behold, I will send my messenger, and he shall prepare the way before me: and the Lord, whom ye seek [Christ], shall suddenly come to his temple, even the messenger of the covenant..." (Malachi 3:1).

It was John the Baptist who prepared the way—but that was before Jesus's FIRST coming. When we read on through verses 2-6 it becomes altogether evident that this prophecy in

Malachi is talking about Christ's *Second* Coming, in power and glory, to RULE.

WHO, then, as a human messenger (one bearing a message) was to prepare the way before His SECOND Coming? And *what of the temple* to which He is to come?

Look briefly at the prophecy of Haggai. It concerns the contingent of Jews who returned to Jerusalem 70 years after the destruction of Solomon's temple to build the second temple on the same site.

The prophecy concerns Zerubbabel, governor of the contingent, and builder of this second temple. This was the same temple to which Jesus did come—except that the Roman King Herod had somewhat enlarged, restored, and embellished it.

But Zerubbabel was merely a TYPE. The prophecy, as we see plainly beginning verse 6, chapter 2, is millennial.

"For thus saith the [Eternal] of hosts; Yet once, it is a little while, and I will shake the heavens, and the earth, and the sea, and the dry land; And I will shake all nations, and the desire [RSV has, 'so that the treasures of all nations shall come'] of all nations shall come: and I will fill this house with glory, saith the [Eternal] of hosts. ... The glory of this latter house shall be greater than of the former ..." (verses 6-7, 9).

It is speaking of the end time—at the Second Coming of Christ.

Now what does it mean, "The glory of this latter house [or *latter-day* house] shall be greater than of the former"?—that is, greater than Solomon's temple, which had the most glorious splendor of any building on Earth? Certainly the second temple, built by Zerubbabel, even though larger, could not *compare* in splendor to Solomon's.

But God was speaking of the temple *to which Christ shall come,* at His glorious Second Coming as King of kings and Lord of lords!

Jesus Christ came the first time still in the days of Old Covenant Israel—a carnal-minded and rebellious people. It was a material temple, even as He came to a physical, carnal people!

But He is coming the second time in supreme power and glory. He will come this time to a GLORIOUS TEMPLE—a SPIRITUAL, not a material, temple!

Of God's Church He says, in the second chapter of Ephesians,

"Now therefore ye are…of the household [Family] of God [the CHURCH]; And are built upon the foundation of the apostles and prophets, Jesus Christ himself being the chief corner stone; In whom *all the building fitly framed together groweth unto an holy temple* in the Lord" (verses 19-21).

The glorified Christ is coming to the glorified temple—with a glory far greater than Solomon's temple!

Note it. Christ is *not* coming to a material building, but to His Church, then to be GLORIFIED with Him!

Notice further, in Ephesians chapter 4: "From whom the whole body [Body of Christ—the Church!] *fitly joined together and compacted by that which every joint supplieth…*" (verse 16).

Now let's UNDERSTAND!

Old Testament Israel, both church and state, lived in the days of the first Adam. They had the one "human" spirit—they were carnal minded, hostile against God, not subject to the law of God. But God gave them His laws (spiritual, as well as sacrificial, ceremonial, and statutory). It proved that without the *second* spirit—the Holy Spirit of God—people would not turn to the right way of life—*even though God revealed to them the knowledge*—not only of Himself—but of His GOVERNMENT!

But the New Testament Church of God started out with God's Holy Spirit added to the "human" spirit, even from its inception.

The Old Testament sacrificial laws and ceremonial rituals were a mere *temporary substitute* for Christ and the Holy Spirit. When the reality came, the substitute was ended—but the basic SPIRITUAL LAW—the law of LOVE, codified in the Ten Commandments—continued. But the CHURCH was required, having the Holy Spirit, to obey them not merely according to the strictness of the letter but according to the spirit—or principal, or obvious intent, of the law (2 Corinthians 3:6).

Now we come to the purpose and function of the Church of God.

Immediately after the foundation of the Church, the apostles Peter and John performed a sensational healing of a well-known cripple—after which Peter preached to the crowd that was attracted (Acts 3:1-26). But immediately the priests, captains of the temple, and Sadducees threw the apostles into prison overnight (Acts 4:1-3). And the next morning the apostles were brought before the high priest and his family beside other rulers and dignitaries. They were severely THREATENED and commanded to cease preaching in the name of Christ.

These apostles were human. This experience was unnerving! They went immediately to a company of CHURCH MEMBERS for encouragement, prayer and morale strengthening (Acts 4:23).

These loyal Church brethren "lifted up their voice to God" (Acts 4:24) in united prayer, petitioning God for inspiration and divine power, that the apostles might continue boldly proclaiming the message.

Notice here an important function of the Church. The Church lay members did not go forth with the message—they *backed up,* unitedly, the apostles who were charged with THE GREAT COMMISSION. Notice: "And when they had prayed, the place was shaken where they were assembled together..." (verse 31).

These Church brethren were able to stand solidly and loyally back of the apostles, because they "were of one heart and of one soul [mind]" (verse 32).

Later, when the savage persecution had set in, the Apostle James was martyred; King Herod also had Peter cast into prison, with the intent probably of killing him also (Acts 12:1-4).

"[B]ut," verse 5, "prayer was made without ceasing of the church unto God for him."

The result? God sent an angel to loose the chains that bound Peter, and to lead him secretly out of the prison. Peter fled on to Caesarea.

THE PREVAILING ERROR

At this point it is well to clarify further a most common and universal erroneous belief. It is the assumption that God is desperately waging a contest against Satan, attempting to get every living human "saved" NOW! This assumption must concede that Satan is winning that contest overwhelmingly! But there is NO SUCH CONTEST. Satan has power to do ONLY what God ALLOWS!

The corollary to this assumption is an even more tragic belief that has acquired universal acceptance. And that is the fallacy that everyone *not* now "saved" is "lost"—condemned to an eternal hell fire—which, incidentally, is also a myth. The vast majority are neither "saved" nor "lost." Just not yet JUDGED!

It was our first human progenitor that made the CHOICE. God accepted his decision, and pronounced sentence on Adam's world for 6,000 years—except for those God called for some special performance. The 6,000-year sentence is about to expire—and a happy, joyful world of PEACE, with eternal life available to all, is now just around the corner!

Jesus Christ emphatically verified this sentence God pronounced on the world. He said plainly, "*NO MAN CAN* come to me, except the Father which hath sent me draw him ..." (John 6:44). And none can come to God, except through Him!

So let us clarify once for all time that the purpose of the Church is definitely NOT to preach or persuade the whole world into a spiritual salvation, NOW—before Christ's Second Coming!

Some have construed the GREAT COMMISSION as being to the Church to fulfill as a whole—to evangelize and "save" the world—NOW! A large system of missionaries from traditional Christianity has resulted.

Examine, now, the three places where THE GREAT COMMISSION is explained.

First, the report of THE GREAT COMMISSION recorded in Matthew 28: "Now the eleven disciples" (Judas already had left them) "went to Galilee, to the mountain to which Jesus had directed them. And when they saw him they worshipped him; but some doubted. And Jesus came and said to them ...." To WHOM? Not the Church as a whole! Only to the disciples who were to become the original APOSTLES! "... 'All authority in heaven and on earth has been given to me. *GO* therefore and make disciples [learners—those taught] of all nations, baptizing them in the name of the Father and of the Son and of the Holy Spirit, teaching them to observe all that I have commanded you; and lo, I am with you always, to the close of the age'" (Matthew 28:16-20, RSV).

Notice carefully. This GREAT COMMISSION to be SENT FORTH with Christ's gospel message was given only to those who were apostles—and the word "apostle" means "one sent forth" with the message!

The King James translation of the above has been MISinterpreted by some to imply that ALL the people in every nation were to be converted *then*.

The King James Version has: "Go ye therefore, and teach all nations, baptizing them....." The sense is, "teach *within* all nations," NOT teaching every individual. The RSV translation, above quoted, also has this same sense. "Make disciples—students—learners—to HEAR the message *within* all nations." And, "baptizing them" can refer ONLY to those God specially *called,* since Christ said plainly, "NO MAN CAN come to me, except the Father which hath sent me draw him."

Now examine Mark's account of THE GREAT COMMISSION (chapter 16). Most translations from the original Greek text into English OMIT verses 9-20, saying these verses were NOT INSPIRED and were added at a later date by uninspired editors. Even so, the RSV does quote these verses in finer type, starting verse 15, as follows: "And he said to them"—the 11 apostles—"Go into all the world and preach the gospel to the whole creation." That is, announce the GOOD NEWS of the coming Kingdom of God. Continue: "He who believes and is baptized will be saved..." (verse 16). But Jesus plainly said NO MAN could come to Christ—believe—except those specially called by the Father!

Notice now the King James translation: "Afterward he [Jesus] appeared unto the eleven as they sat at meat .... And he said unto them, Go ye into all the world, and preach the gospel to every creature. He that believeth and is baptized shall be saved ..." (Mark 16:14-16). Of course NONE could believe and be baptized EXCEPT those God the Father specially called. So there is NOWHERE ANY CONTRADICTION. The GREAT COMMISSION was given to the APOSTLES—those "sent forth" with the message—NOT the lay members of the Church.

What, then? Did not the lay members have any part in proclaiming the gospel? Definitely they did, as we have seen. Their part was to *back up* the apostles—stand behind them with their prayers, encouragement, tithes and offerings. They are PART OF A WELL-ORGANIZED TEAM, as we shall show in more detail.

And there is NO EVIDENCE in either Matthew's account or Mark's that any were to be baptized *except* those God the Father had called to a special service.

But NOTHING contradicts the fact that God had withdrawn His Holy Spirit from ALL, *except* those specially called.

Now notice the account in Matthew 24. This is in the form of a prophecy, for our present living generation:

The King James has, "And this gospel of the kingdom shall be preached in all the world for a witness unto all nations; and then shall the end [of this age] come" (Matthew 24:14).

The RSV is the same in meaning: "And this gospel of the kingdom will be preached throughout the whole world, as a testimony to all nations; and then the end will come."

THE CHURCH AN ORGANIZED BODY

Is the Church of God merely a scattered, isolated, number of professing Christians, each going his own way to get out the gospel—or, as many believe, to GET his personal salvation and eternal life?

Jesus Christ specially called His disciples, trained them to become His apostles. To THEM—the apostles—the ones "sent forth" with His gospel message—He gave THE GREAT COMMISSION—*not* to the laity of the Church as a whole.

But WHAT OF GOD'S CHURCH? HOW IS IT ORGANIZED? It is a spiritual organism—but also it is PHYSICALLY ORGANIZED, as we shall now see.

The Church is the begotten Family—or household—of God (Ephesians 2:19), "And are built upon the FOUNDATION of the apostles and prophets, Jesus Christ himself being the chief corner stone" (Ephesians 2:20).

It is, continues verse 21, like a "building fitly framed together [which] groweth unto an holy TEMPLE in the Lord."

It is the TEMPLE to which Christ shall come at His Second Coming in GLORY! It is that Body of Christ that is the affianced BRIDE of Christ, to be married to Him (as the Old Covenant was a marriage covenant) when He returns.

Ephesians says: "...Christ also loved the church, and gave himself for it.... That he might present it to himself a GLORIOUS CHURCH" (Ephesians 5:25-27) in the resurrection!

Of that same marriage, Revelation says: "Alleluia: for the Lord God omnipotent reigneth. Let us be glad and rejoice, and give honour to him: for the MARRIAGE of the Lamb [Christ] is come, and his wife [the resurrected glorified Church] hath made herself ready" (Revelation 19:6-7).

It is not only a SPIRITUAL ORGANISM—it is a well-organized physical ORGANIZATION! Notice 1 Corinthians 12: "...brethren, I would not have you ignorant" (verse 1). "But now are they many members, YET BUT ONE BODY" (verse 20).

And it is a well-ORGANIZED body (verses 4-6, 11-12): "Now there are diversities of gifts, but the same Spirit. And there are *differences of administrations,* but the same Lord. And there are *diversities of operations,* but it is the same God which worketh all in all. ... But all these worketh that one and the selfsame Spirit, dividing to every man severally *as he will.* For ... the body is ONE"—united, organized into cooperative team-work—not scattered individuals, each claiming to serve God *in his own way!*

Continuing: "For ... the body is ONE, and hath many members, and all the members of that ONE BODY, being many, are ONE BODY: so also is Christ. For by ONE SPIRIT are we all baptized into one body .... That there should be no schism [division] in the body; but that the members should have the same care [that is, outgoing concern and love] one for another" (verses 12-13, 25).

Continuing: "And God hath set some in the church, first apostles, secondarily prophets, thirdly teachers, after that miracles, then gifts of healing, helps, governments, diversities of tongues" (verse 28).

Now back to Ephesians. What about the member who GOES OUT OF THE CHURCH, to have his *own* relationship with Christ— to *GET* his own salvation? He is OUTSIDE the Body of Christ!

Notice, again, the "household of God"—the CHURCH— is built upon a FOUNDATION. Would one build a BUILDING on a foundation of shifting sand? God's Church is built upon "the FOUNDATION of the apostles [the New Testament], and prophets [Old Testament, whose prophecies are for US TODAY (1 Corinthians 10:11)], Jesus Christ himself being the chief corner stone" (Ephesians 2:19-20).

How WELL ORGANIZED?

"In whom all the building [the Church] fitly framed together groweth unto an holy TEMPLE in the Lord" (verse 21).

Further: "From whom the whole body *fitly joined together* and compacted by that which every joint supplieth, according to the effectual working in the measure of *every part,* maketh

increase of the body unto the edifying of itself in love"
(Ephesians 4:16).

Yes, Christ ORGANIZED His Church.

"And his gifts were that some should be apostles, some
prophets, some evangelists, some pastors and teachers"
(verse 11, RSV), continuing in KJV: "For the perfecting of the
saints, for the work of the ministry, for the edifying of the
body of Christ: Till *we all come in the unity of the faith,* and of
the knowledge of the Son of God, unto a perfect man, unto the
measure of the stature of the fulness of Christ" (verses 12-13).

What about a single member, "a joint, or part," going off by
itself—or following a MAN instead of the CHURCH OF GOD that
is in direct continuous succession from the apostolic Church
founded by Christ, in A.D. 31? He is like a joint or a piece of
wood or stone, entirely outside of, and therefore NO PART OF,
the BODY OF CHRIST that shall MARRY Christ!

We have seen that Christ gave the lay body of the Church
the SPECIAL MISSION to *back up* His apostles in their GOING FORTH
with the gospel to the world—with their prayers, encouragement, tithes and offerings.

But this GIVING of their prayers, encouragement and financial support was GOD'S ASSIGNMENT *as the very means* of developing in *them* God's holy, righteous CHARACTER—that they,
with the apostles and evangelists, may qualify to RULE with
and under Christ in God's Kingdom. This *very means* of character development within the laity is THE WAY OF *GIVING*—not
Satan's way of GETTING.

God's WAY—the WAY of His law—is GIVING of outflowing
LOVE. It is the GIVING way. The person who tries to be an individual separate Christian, to GET his own salvation, is going at
it the GETTING way—*Satan's way.* And I would not want to try
to GET myself into God's Kingdom by Satan's way.

Notice again WHY God set apostles, evangelists, pastors and
other elders in His Church NOT ONLY for the work of the ministry, being SENT FORTH into all the world announcing Christ's
message of HOPE. Read it again (verses 12-13): It was "[f]or
the perfecting of the saints ... for the edifying [enlightening—
instructing] of the body of Christ: TILL we all come in the
UNITY of the faith, and of the KNOWLEDGE of the Son of God,
unto a perfect man ...."

But cannot a single separate individual EDIFY HIMSELF, *outside* of the Church? Not likely—and THAT IS NOT GOD'S WAY.

How does God infuse HIS TRUTH into the Church? NOT through each individual separately—but through the apostles, and other ministers under them.

In the time of the first apostles—first century—the Bible was not yet completely written. God used a very few prophets, through whom He communicated. The prophets gave the message to an apostle. Today the Bible is complete.

However, the laity of the first-century Church received their teaching and instruction from *the apostles*. The original 12 had been taught by Christ in person—and so also had Paul. Jesus Christ was the *personal* Word of God. The Bible is the *written* Word of God. It's all the precise same TRUTH and TEACHING, whether from Jesus in person, when on Earth, or from the written Word of God. God's apostle for our day was taught by the written Word of God—the SAME IDENTICAL TEACHING!

But what of the separated *individual* believer, who tries to GET his salvation all by himself—or by following some MAN, or any of hundreds of professing Christian denominations of our day? He is CUT OFF from that TRUE teaching which Christ reveals to and through His apostle!

What if one in the Church *disagrees* on some point of doctrine? Then he is out of harmony with God's Church. And GOD HAS ONLY THE *ONE* CHURCH.

And all in the Church are commanded to speak the same thing—and it *must* be what CHRIST, either in person, or by written Word, has taught His apostle.

To the Church at Corinth, the Apostle Paul wrote: "Now I beseech you, brethren, by the name of our Lord Jesus Christ, that ye all *speak the same thing...*" (1 Corinthians 1:10). Some of them wanted to follow Peter, some wanted to follow Apollos, some Paul. But PAUL was their apostle, and Christ taught them by PAUL.

The separated individual believer will follow *his own* idea of God's truth. THAT IS NOT GOD'S WAY.

God in His almighty wisdom has raised up the CHURCH as HIS MEANS of teaching all the SAME TRUTH—all speaking the SAME THING! Not each individual *his own thing!*

God raised up the CHURCH, *not only* that its apostles and

evangelists go into all the world announcing the GOOD NEWS of the coming Kingdom of God, but also, as *the very means* for the general body of lay members to develop God's own holy righteous CHARACTER—by means of *GIVING*—giving their continuous prayers for the apostle, *giving* their encouragement, tithes and offerings!

WHAT, then, of the person who follows after a man outside the Church—or tries to GET his salvation, simply by GETTING—and not GIVING that which members are to give to the Church's work? Consider Jesus's parable of the pounds in Luke 19. The pound is the British unit of money. Jesus illustrated Himself giving each member, on conversion, "one pound"—representing the Holy Spirit given at conversion. But the Christian MUST GROW in grace and Christ's knowledge. As he does, by GIVING in the Church, he receives an increasing amount of God's Spirit. The isolated, separated member will probably LOSE OUT (see Luke 19:20-24).

IN SUMMARY: WHY THE CHURCH?

Finally, WHY the Church? WHY did not Christ just "save" separated individuals? What is the REAL PURPOSE OF THE CHURCH?

Like most everything in the Bible, the purpose and function of the Church has been grossly misunderstood. The entire world has been deceived by Satan (Revelation 12:9).

Jesus had not come on a "soul-saving crusade." The most widespread false assumption of all is that Christ is contesting against Satan to "get everybody saved NOW!" And with it, the supposition that all not saved are "LOST"—condemned! They are neither. They are not yet JUDGED!

But in Adam, by his decision, all humanity has been *sentenced* to 6,000 years of being completely cut off from God! That is, all except the comparative very few specifically called for a special mission.

Jesus Christ, I repeat, emphatically verified this 6,000-year sentence (John 6:44). No scripture can or does contradict that plain statement of Jesus.

Jesus called, chose, and for 3½ years trained His apostles to become, with Him and the prophets, the FOUNDATION on which the Church was built. Also He set the example, those 3½ years, for His apostles, in proclaiming (announcing) the coming KINGDOM OF GOD. Then Christ died for the sins of humanity, and was resurrected, and ascended to God's throne in heaven.

On the day of Pentecost, A.D. 31, He sent the Holy Spirit in a great manifestation both visible and audible, to found His Church.

On that day of Pentecost, it was Peter, chief apostle, who proclaimed the gospel message—and that day God ADDED 3,000 baptized that same day.

A day or so later—very possibly the very next day—Peter and John healed the cripple and Peter preached the gospel. God ADDED another 2,000 to the Church.

It is significant, and generally unrealized, that neither Jesus nor the apostles embarked on any "soul-saving crusade," which is a modern Protestant practice. The apostles, as Jesus had done, proclaimed the gospel—the GOOD NEWS of a coming BETTER WORLD. It was not an emotional pleading, "Won't you give your heart to the Lord?"

True, because unbelieving Jews did not accept Jesus as their promised Messiah, the apostles, at first, put special emphasis on the fact they were eye-witnesses to Jesus's Messiahship and resurrection. They had been with Him 3½ years before He was crucified, and 40 days after He rose from the dead.

But they did proclaim the same message Jesus had taught them—the coming Kingdom of God. It was not a begging for "souls." "[T]he Lord *added* to the church daily such as should be saved" (Acts 2:47).

When the apostles met with fierce persecution, imprisonment and threat, the laity of the Church ENCOURAGED them, prayed heartrendingly for them, supported them financially.

So, let the truth be clarified once for all, the PURPOSE of the Church was NOT to "get the world saved NOW!"

God's PURPOSE in raising up His Church in a world otherwise CUT OFF from God was dual:

1) To provide a united body of Spirit-led believers to back up the apostles (and evangelists) who had been specially trained to GO FORTH into all the world with Christ's gospel message. All this, as *their part* in THE GREAT COMMISSION. Theirs was a WORK OF *GIVING*—giving of their prayers—their encouragement, and financial support of the ORGANIZED gospel

WORK. And this *as GOD's means of, and the training ground for,*

2) the overcoming of Satan, and the constant development of that holy, righteous CHARACTER—thus qualifying them to sit with Christ on the throne of Earthwide GOVERNMENT.

GOD'S WAY of developing His holy character was THE *GIVING* WAY. GOD's way of life is the GIVING way of outgoing LOVE. Satan's way is INCOMING self-advantage—hostility to God's way and to His Church.

Those who allow an attitude of hostility and rebellion against God's Church—and God's GOVERNMENT within His Church—to cause them to leave, and "go it alone," or follow a MAN, are seeking merely TO GET salvation FOR THE SELF! That is NOT God's WAY!

THE GLORY ON BEYOND!

Happily, the 6,000-year sentence on Adam's world—being *cut off* from God—is due to END in our present living generation. This world, now—still Satan's world except for God's CHURCH—is fast plunging into the supreme CRISIS of world tribulation. But it is said to be "darkest just before dawn!"

Then, SUDDENLY, when least expected by the "cut-off world," Jesus Christ will come in supreme supernatural POWER AND GLORY! Yes, "at such an hour as ye think not," said Jesus.

His CHURCH will have been made ready!

"For this we say unto you by the word of the Lord, that we which are alive and remain unto the coming of the Lord shall not [precede] them which are asleep [dead]. For the Lord himself shall descend from heaven with a shout, with the voice of the archangel, and with the trump of God: and the dead in Christ shall rise first: Then we which are alive and remain shall be caught up together with them in the clouds, to meet the Lord in the air: and so shall we ever be with the Lord" (1 Thessalonians 4:15-17). He is coming to RULE ALL THE EARTH!

Then shall be fulfilled Revelation 19:6-7: the mighty voice of the archangel shouting, "ALLELUIA: for the Lord God omnipotent reigneth. Let us be glad and rejoice"! The Church, resurrected IN GLORY, shall reign with Christ a thousand years!

Satan will be banished! God will call ALL LIVING to His salvation. After the Millennium shall come the GREAT WHITE

THRONE JUDGEMENT (Revelation 20:11-12) when all who had been cut off from God for 6,000 years shall be resurrected MORTAL—and all called to God's salvation and eternal life!

Then, the glorious eternity beyond—all saints then immortal, *inheriting* the transcendent human potential—RENEWING THE FACE OF ALL DECAYED PLANETS, FINISHING THE GLORIOUS BEAUTIFUL CREATION THROUGHOUT THE WHOLE ENDLESS UNIVERSE—in happiness, joy and GLORY!

Chapter 10
Just What Do You Mean ... Conversion?

HOW MANY TIMES HAVE YOU HEARD NON-CHRISTIANS, JUDGING one who professes Christ, say in disgust: "Well if *that's* Christianity, I don't want any of it!"

How many judge GOD by the way professing Christians live? How many assume that one must live a *perfect* life, before he can become a Christian?

How many say: "If I could give up smoking, I'd become a Christian."

How many think a Christian is supposed to be perfect, never doing anything wrong? Suppose you do see or hear about a Christian doing something WRONG. Does that mean he is a hypocrite—that he is *not* really a Christian, after all?

Is it possible for one to actually SIN while he is a Christian and *still remain* a truly converted Christian?

The startling TRUTH is that few know just what *is* a Christian. Few know HOW one is converted—whether suddenly, all at once, or gradually. Does conversion happen *immediately*, or is it a PROCESS? IT'S HIGH TIME WE UNDERSTAND what constitutes REAL CONVERSION.

Do Christians ever sin? If one does, is he "lost"?

First let me ask—and answer the question, "What is true Christian conversion?" "What is a real Christian in the sight of God?" Does joining a church make one a Christian? Does saying, "I accept the Lord Jesus Christ as my Savior" make one a Christian?

Let's get the Bible definition. In Romans 8:6-9 you will read: "For to be carnally minded is death; but to be spiritually minded is life and peace. Because the carnal mind [fleshly mind] is enmity [hostile] against God: for it is not subject to the law of God, neither indeed can be. So then they that are in the flesh [fleshly *minded*] cannot please God. But ye are not in the flesh, but in the Spirit, if so be that the Spirit of God dwell in you. Now if any man have not the Spirit of Christ, he is none of his."

A Christian, then, is one who has received, and in whose mind dwells, the Holy Spirit of God. Otherwise he is NOT Christ's—NOT a Christian.

FALSE CONVERSION

Millions may *profess* to be Christians, but *unless* God's Holy Spirit, given as HIS GIFT by GRACE, is at the moment dwelling in them, they are NOT CHRISTIANS.

Millions may have their names written in church membership books, and still be "NONE OF HIS"—not really CHRISTIANS at all! And millions are *so* deceived (Revelation 12:9).

SO UNDERSTAND THIS! A person is a Christian—in God's sight—ONLY while God's Holy Spirit is dwelling IN him. Not before! Not after!

So a truly *converted* person has received (and currently has) God's Holy Spirit dwelling within him. But, there is yet quite a bit more to understanding what constitutes real conversion.

REAL CONVERSION

There is a sense in which true conversion *does* take place at a *definite time*—all at once. But it is also true that in another sense conversion is *worked out gradually*—a process of development and growth.

NOW NOTICE CAREFULLY!

WHEN does one really become a Christian? It is when he receives God's Holy Spirit. In Romans 8:9, we read that unless we have the Holy Spirit, we are not Christ's—not Christians.

There is a definite TIME when God's Spirit enters into one. At the *very moment* he receives the Holy Spirit, he is, in this first sense, *converted*. Yes, *all at once!* If he has Christ's Spirit, he is CHRIST'S—he is a Christian! The very *Life* of God has entered into (impregnated) him. He has been begotten as a child of God.

But does that mean his salvation is complete? Is he now fully and finally "saved"? Is that all there is to it? Is he now, suddenly, *perfect?* Is it now impossible for him to do WRONG?

No! FAR FROM IT! BUT WHY? What's the answer? Why do so many MISunderstand?

Why does almost NOBODY understand the very PURPOSE of the Christian life?

THE PURPOSE OF THE CHRISTIAN LIFE

WHY do people not understand the very gospel Jesus Christ taught? He taught the KINGDOM OF GOD. So did the apostles, including Paul. Jesus spoke mostly in parables. Take a quick look at one or two. Notice what Jesus revealed. Notice the awe-inspiring TREMENDOUS potential that is ours.

Take the parable of the nobleman going to a far country, later to return. It is in Luke 19:11-27. Jesus is the nobleman. He was going to a far country—to the heaven of God's throne, seat of the government of the entire universe. He spoke this parable because His disciples thought the Kingdom of God should appear immediately. So far more than 1,900 years have gone by, and the Kingdom of God has not yet appeared.

So He called, in the parable, His 10 servants, and He gave them 10 pounds—a pound each, using, in our English-language translation, the English unit of money. This is symbolic of one unit of SPIRITUAL VALUE with which each was started out. In other words, representative of the portion of God's Holy Spirit which was given to each on initial conversion.

But His citizens hated Him. They rejected Him as their RULER. They said, "We will not have this man to REIGN OVER US" (verse 14). The Kingdom of God is a RULING GOVERNMENT. They, as of then, received no conversion—no "pounds." (They shall yet find conversion, as many, many passages of Scripture affirm.)

Now the reason for His going to heaven was to "receive for himself a KINGDOM, and to return" (verse 12). That is, He was going to the throne of the government of the entire universe where God Almighty, the Father, sits, to have conferred on Him the RULERSHIP OF THE WORLD. The coronation ceremony will take place in heaven, at the throne of UNIVERSE RULE. When He returns He will be crowned with MANY CROWNS (Revelation 19:12). He is coming to RULE ALL NATIONS with almighty divine POWER (verse 15).

Back to Luke 19. On his return, his servants, to whom he had given the money—that is, the beginning unit of GOD'S SPIRIT at conversion—are to be called to an accounting, "that he might know how much every man had GAINED" while he was gone (verse 15). This means each Christian is expected to GROW spiritually—in spiritual KNOWLEDGE and grace (see 2 Peter 3:18). The Christian life is a life of spiritual GOING TO SCHOOL—of training for a POSITION IN GOD'S KINGDOM, when and after we shall be changed from mortal to immortal—when we shall be no longer flesh-and-blood humans, but composed of SPIRIT, with eternal life inherent.

In the parable, the first came to report he had multiplied what he had been given TEN TIMES. You see, the receiving of God's Spirit is GOD'S GIFT—that is what God does—it comes by GRACE, as a gift. WE CAN'T EARN IT. But all through the New Testament it is made plain we shall be REWARDED according to OUR WORKS. Not SAVED by works we have done. This man had, by his own application, multiplied his spiritual gift 10 times—his one pound was now 10 pounds. He received a greater REWARD than the one who gained five pounds.

The nobleman (Christ) said to him, "Well, thou good servant: because thou hast been faithful in a very little, have thou AUTHORITY over TEN CITIES" (Luke 19:17).

He had qualified to RULE. He had been obedient to God's commands—God's government. We have to BE RULED before we can learn to RULE.

The second servant had increased his spiritual stock of goods five times. He had qualified, in this life, for HALF as much as the first servant. He was given HALF the REWARD.

THE KINGDOM OF GOD

So the parable of the pounds shows Christians are to RULE under Christ, *when* the Kingdom of God is set up. Jesus was speaking of GOVERNMENT—*world government*. This parable was given to show that the Kingdom of God was not to appear at that time. The Kingdom is *not* an ethereal, sentimental something "in our hearts." It is *not* the Church.

Daniel's prophecy shows that the SAINTS are to RULE, under Christ the Messiah, when He sets up literal WORLD GOVERNMENT. See Daniel 2—read it through and then notice verse 44. This Kingdom will break in pieces every other form of government— all rule of man—and will stand forever. Notice Daniel 7—and especially verses 18 and 22. It will be an earthly Kingdom—not in heaven, but "UNDER the whole heaven," verse 27.

Jesus said: "And he that overcometh, and keepeth MY WORKS unto the end, to him will I give POWER over the nations: And he shall RULE THEM with a rod of iron..." (Revelation 2:26-27).

He said, "To him that overcometh will I grant to sit with me in my throne, even as I also overcame, and am set down with my Father in his throne" (Revelation 3:21). When Jesus said this, through John in the 90s A.D., He was in heaven with His Father on the throne from which the entire universe is governed.

When Jesus sits on His own throne on this Earth it will be the throne of David, in Jerusalem. Notice what is said of Jesus: "He shall be great, and shall be called the Son of the Highest: and the [Eternal] God shall give unto him the throne of his father David: And he shall REIGN over the house of Jacob for ever; and of his kingdom there shall be no end" (Luke 1:32-33).

But He was not going to set up the world government of the Kingdom of God *at that time.* The Bible speaks of *three* worlds—or *ages*—in time order. First, the world that then was, overflowed with water—prior to the Flood; second, this present evil world; and third, the world to come. On trial for His life before Pilate, Jesus said He was born to be a king (John 18:37), but that His kingdom was "not of this world." He will rule THE WORLD TOMORROW (verse 36).

The saints (Spirit-led Christians) are to reign, under Christ, "ON THE EARTH" (Revelation 5:10), for a thousand years (Revelation 20:4, 6).

WHY has the whole world been deceived with a false gospel? (Revelation 12:9). WHY have they been deceived into belief in a counterfeit Kingdom of God? (Request our free book *Mystery of the Ages.*)

Look again at the many parables of Jesus. They teach the Kingdom of God. They make plain the fact the Kingdom of God is the WORLD GOVERNMENT soon, now, to be set up by Christ, coming in ALL POWER and GLORY, to bring us world peace, abundance, happiness and joy.

The purpose of the Christian life is to train future KINGS to rule with and under Christ. How then, does one become a Christian? When? And WHY is salvation a PROCESS, as well as an initial phase when he becomes a Christian instantaneously?

Here is the PLAIN TRUTH you need to know.

REAL REPENTANCE

I repeat: "A Christian [a truly converted person] is one who has received, and in whose mind dwells the Holy Spirit of God."

But how does one receive the Spirit of God?

On the day the Church of God was started, the Apostle Peter said, "Repent, and be baptized … in the name of Jesus Christ for the remission of sins, and ye shall receive the gift of the Holy [Spirit]" (Acts 2:38).

Repent of what? Of sin. And what is sin? "[S]in is the transgression of the law" (1 John 3:4). What law? The law that the carnal mind, hostile to God, is not subject to—the law of God (Romans 8:7). Again, we read of "the Holy [Spirit], whom God hath given to them that obey him" (Acts 5:32).

These are the two *conditions* to receiving God's GIFT of the Holy Spirit: *repentance* and *faith*. Being baptized is the outward manifestation of the inner faith in Christ. Repentance is not merely being sorry for something one has done—or even many such sins. It is a real repentance of what one *is* and *has been*—of his whole past attitude and life apart from God. It is a total *change* of mind and heart and direction of life. It is a *change* to a new WAY OF LIFE. It is a turning from the *self*-centered way of vanity, selfishness, greed, hostility to authority, envy, jealousy and unconcern for the good and welfare of others to the God-centered WAY of obedience, submission to authority, love toward God *more* than love of self and of love and concern for other humans equal to self-concern.

LOVE is the fulfilling of God's law (Romans 13:10)—but God's law is a *spiritual* law (Romans 7:14) and can be fulfilled only by "the love of God...shed abroad in our hearts by the Holy [Spirit]" (Romans 5:5).

The Holy Spirit will open one's mind to UNDERSTAND God's instruction on how to live, but it will not force one to live God's way—it will not pull or push one. Each Christian must take his own initiative, though God's Spirit will give him help, faith and power. But it is "as many as are *led by* the Spirit of God, they are the sons of God" (Romans 8:14).

REAL CHRISTIAN CONVERSION

The two above-mentioned conditions to becoming a Christian—REPENTANCE and FAITH—we ourselves must perform.

But these do not make us Christians—do not convert us. It is what GOD does—giving His Holy Spirit by His grace as His free gift—that converts us.

Our repentance and faith do not *earn* the receiving of God's Spirit. God does not give us His Spirit *because* we repent and believe. He gives His Spirit *because* He *wants* to give it. He *wants* us to have His Spirit as His gift *before* we repent. He merely *requires* repentance and faith as *conditions*.

Yet no one can, of himself, say: "Oh now, I see—I must repent. All right, I hereby repent." One does not just decide casually, as a matter of routine, to repent. WHY?

Jesus Christ said that none can come to Him, except the Spirit of the Father draw him (John 6:44, 65). God *grants* repentance (Romans 2:4). God calls one, and convicts the mind and conscience by His Spirit, working on the mind externally. Usually a real a struggle goes on within. The person has been shaken to *know* he has done wrong—that he *is* wrong—he has sinned—he *is* a sinner! He is brought to real REPENTANCE, not only for what he has done, but for what he now sees that he *is*. It is not easy. The *self* never wants to die. To *repent* is to make an *unconditional surrender* to God—to *obey His law!*

Yet he, himself, must make the decision. If he does repent, surrender to God, and in FAITH accept Jesus Christ as personal Savior, then, upon performance of these TWO conditions, God *promises* to put within him the GIFT of the Holy Spirit. This is the very *life* of God—SPIRIT life. It imparts to him the very *divine nature!*

Then *what*, at that stage, *has happened?*

This new convert has only been *begotten* of God—not yet BORN. Many who believe they are *"born again"* on receiving the Holy Spirit are more in error in terminology than in what happens. (For a full explanation, write for our free booklet *Just What Do You Mean—Born Again?*)

This new convert has not received the full measure of God's Spirit which Christ had; he is only a *spiritual babe* in Christ. He must now GROW spiritually, just as a newly conceived embryo in its mother's womb must grow physically large enough to be BORN as a human.

This new convert has now REPENTED, in his mind, from the depths of his heart. HE MEANS IT, too! In all sincerity, in his mind and heart, he has *turned around to go the other way*—to live a different life. He is now a CHRISTIAN—he has received God's Holy Spirit. He has *been converted.* He is a Christian. He really *wants* to do what is right—to obey God—to live GOD'S WAY.

WHAT IF A CHRISTIAN SINS?

So a Christian convert, then, is one who has received God's Spirit, which is dwelling in him, leading him, and he is following GOD'S WAY of life. A converted Christian has forsaken his former habitual way of life—his selfish way unconcerned with God. Now he lives in the habitual way of God's Word—in the light of the Word of God.

But suppose, like an 8- or 10-month-old baby trying to learn to walk, as he "walks" this NEW WAY, he stumbles, "falls down," as it were, and SINS. Is he then condemned—lost—no longer a Christian?

I would like you, now, to notice, and UNDERSTAND, what the Apostle John was inspired to write for our admonition. It is in the first letter (epistle) of John:

Speaking of Christ, in his opening salutation, as "[t]hat which was from the beginning...which was with the Father, and was manifested unto us; That which we have seen and heard declare we unto you, that ye also may have fellowship with us: and truly our fellowship is with the Father, and with his Son Jesus Christ" (1 John 1:1-3).

The true Christian has been reconciled to God through

Christ. And, having God's Spirit, he enjoys actual *fellowship* with the Father and the Son Jesus Christ. And even his fellowship with fellow Christians is through God and Christ. He is joined to them, as the different branches are joined to a grape vine and joined together through and by the vine. Compare Jesus's analogy in John 15:1-7. Christians, then, are actually *walking* with Christ—and two cannot walk together except they be in agreement (Amos 3:3).

Now continue in 1 John 1: "This then is the message which we have heard of him, and declare unto you, that God is light, and in him is no darkness at all. If we say that we have fellowship with him, and walk in darkness, we lie, and do not [are not doing] the truth" (verses 5-6). That is, He—the living Christ—is walking in the light—as if on a brilliantly lighted path. But if we are walking in darkness, we are walking on a different path altogether, where it is dark. Therefore we are not walking *with* Him at all, and if we say we are, we are lying.

But suppose, while walking with Him—in the light—one of us stumbles and falls down. This is not a case of having turned away from Him and the path He is treading, to a different and darkened path. If we say, "Oh I'm sorry," would He not give us a hand and help us get up and continue on the lighted path with Him? Would He become angry and say, "Get off my path—go walk down a darkened path"?

In still other words, the true Christian has turned from his former life of habitual sin—and from his former attitude of selfishness and self-seeking when he had no serious intention of living God's way. But now he has turned from his former way. His life, in general, now, is the habitual way of the Christian life.

But he is not perfect the minute he is converted and receives God's Spirit. He must GROW spiritually, in grace and knowledge of Christ, as Peter writes in 2 Peter 3:18. He is the creature of habit, and all old former habits do not just automatically leave him without any effort on his part to overcome them. He must learn to *overcome* sin. It is inevitable that he may be caught off guard and make a mistake. So continue in 1 John 1:

"But if we walk in the light"—that is, even though we may stumble occasionally, it is now only the occasional slip—not a turning our back on God's WAY—*not* a turning back to the *habitual* and constant way of sin.

Do you begin to UNDERSTAND the difference? The true Christian *intends* to live God's WAY. He *wants* to live God's way. He *tries* to live God's way. And, in general, it now actually is his habitual NEW WAY of life. The occasional slip, or sin, does not mean that in his mind and heart he has rejected God and God's WAY. Continue:

"[A]s he is in the light"—if that is now our goal and purpose and habitual way of life—then "we have fellowship one with another, and the blood of Jesus Christ his Son cleanseth us [us who are now Christians] from all sin. If we [Christians] say that we have no sin, we deceive ourselves, and the truth is not in us" (verses 7-8).

If we, now Christians, say that we are already perfect—that we never slip up and make a mistake or commit a sin—we are deceiving ourselves. I knew a woman who deceived herself in this way. She claimed to be above sin—claimed she *never* sinned. And although she was what most people would call a *good* woman, she actually was committing the biggest sin of all—spiritual pride and vanity! She gloried in her "sinless" state. She lacked Christian humility.

But if, while walking down this *lighted* path with God, one stumbles and falls down, does God kick him aside?

Verse 9: "If we [we who are Christians—it is *not* talking about the unconverted] confess our sins, he is faithful and just to forgive us our sins, and to cleanse us from all unrighteousness."

So notice the "IF." "If we *confess* our sins." When we stumble, we must admit it—we must repent of it—we must ask forgiveness. If we deny it, or blame it on somebody else, we shall not be forgiven. We must confess it—to God!

"If we say that we [as Christians] have not sinned, we make him a liar, and his word is not in us" (verse 10). The context continues right on into the second chapter: "My little children, these things write I unto you, that ye sin not." In other words, we *should* not sin—we must strive to avoid any sin. God gives us no license to sin. But, "... if any man sin, we [we Christians] have an advocate with the Father, Jesus Christ the righteous: And he is the propitiation for our sins [those of us who are Christians]: and not for ours only, but also for the sins of the whole world" (1 John 2:1-2). But, of course He is the propitiation for the sins of the unconverted in the world *only* when they come to real repentance, and faith in Christ.

REAL CONVERSION—A PROCESS

Because many do not correctly understand the whole above-mentioned process, they become discouraged. And some even give up even trying to live a Christian life. And WHY? *Because of the false notion that a Christian is one who becomes* PERFECT *at one fell swoop,* or that one cannot become a Christian *until* he has broken all wrong habits, and *made himself* righteous.

It's vital to UNDERSTAND how true Christianity REALLY WORKS!

The newly begotten Christian must grow up, spiritually. What would you think of a human baby, who became 6 feet tall *all at once,* without growing up? The growing-up process requires TIME. There is an *instant* when a person receives the impregnating Holy Spirit of God—when he first becomes a Christian. But he is only a spiritual infant. He must *grow up* spiritually.

The newly converted person, *in his mind* and *heart,* sincerely has ABOUT-FACED! He has actually gained contact with GOD, and received God's Holy Spirit. God's own divine NATURE has now been conceived within him. BUT THAT'S ALL: It is *merely conceived*—not yet full grown! He is still human—mortal—flesh and blood. He is still composed of matter, not spirit.

Understand this!

For nearly 6,000 years, humanity has been going in the WAY OF pride and vanity, selfishness and greed, a lack of outgoing concern for others—the spirit of competition, opposition, strife, effort to acquire, and to exalt the self. Humans have been filled with self-gratification, jealousy, envy, resentment toward others, a spirit of rebellion against authority and hostility toward God and the law of God.

The Christian must overcome these tendencies.

The Christian must develop the righteous CHARACTER to choose the right way, and resist the wrong—to discipline the *self* in the way he ought to go, instead of the way of self-desire and vanity.

PERFECT CHARACTER

God's PURPOSE in having created humanity—in having caused YOU to be born—is to reproduce Himself. (Write for our free booklet *God Is a Family.*)

God, above all things, *is* PERFECT, RIGHTEOUS CHARACTER! God is able to create character within us; but it must be done as a result of our independent free choice. We, as individual separate entities, have our part in the process.

What *is* perfect character? It is the ability, in a separate entity with free moral agency, to come to the KNOWLEDGE of the right from the wrong—the true from the false—and to CHOOSE the right, and possess the WILL to enforce self-discipline to DO the right and resist the wrong.

Like muscle, character is developed, and grows by exercise. My name is Armstrong. I suppose I could make my arm slightly stronger, and develop the muscle, by constantly bending it back and forth at the elbow. But if I pull, or push, against some heavy weight or resistance, the muscle will develop much faster. There is within us this NATURE that exerts a heavy pull *against* that perfect righteous character—to give us something to *strive against* for the VERY PURPOSE OF STRENGTHENING AND DEVELOPING RIGHT CHARACTER!

God's CHARACTER travels in the direction of His law—the way of LOVE. It is an outgoing CONCERN for others. God has that character! He has an outgoing concern for you and for me. He GAVE His only begotten Son to reconcile us to Him and make the JOYS of His character and everlasting life possible for us (John 3:16). He showers on us every good and precious gift. He even puts within us HIS DIVINE NATURE (2 Peter 1:4)—*when* we repent and turn from the WRONG ways of THIS WORLD, begin to *resist* it, and turn TO Him through faith in Jesus Christ as personal Savior!

God's divine nature is the nature of love—of giving, serving, helping—of outgoing concern. It is also the nature of humility.

Now when one is converted—has repented, and *turned from* this world's false WAYS—has *at once* received God's Holy Spirit—his humanity—his HUMAN nature does not flee. It was (probably subconsciously) injected within us by Satan, the prince of the power of the air. He *still* exerts a pull. We still live in THIS PRESENT EVIL WORLD, and *it* exerts a pull. God still allows Satan to be around. And Satan *is* still around!

So we now have THREE PULLS TO RESIST—to OVERCOME! We must now *overcome* these three: Satan, this world, and our own SELVES. We have to battle against these three, in order to develop and strengthen RIGHT CHARACTER within us. God says plainly it is THE OVERCOMERS who shall be saved—who shall REIGN with Christ! (Revelation 2:26-27; 3:21; 21:7).

GOD'S HELP

No human being is strong enough to do this BY HIMSELF! He must seek, and IN FAITH receive, the help and power of GOD. Even with God's power he will not overcome such forces easily or all at once. IT IS NOT EASY! Christ plainly said the way to ultimate salvation is hard, difficult (Matthew 7:13-14). It's a constant BATTLE—a struggle against self, the world, and the devil. The creation of CHARACTER comes through EXPERIENCE. It takes TIME!

This development is a PROCESS. It is a matter of GROWTH—DEVELOPMENT. It requires, to become PERFECT, full and right KNOWLEDGE of the very Word of God; because Jesus taught that we must *live by* EVERY WORD OF GOD (Matthew 4:4; Luke 4:4).

The natural, unconverted mind cannot fully and rightly UNDERSTAND the Scriptures of God. But the Holy Spirit *opens* the mind to this spiritual comprehension. The acquisition of this KNOWLEDGE, in itself, is a procedure requiring TIME. It is the DOERS of this Word, not hearers only, who shall be saved (Romans 2:13).

But can any man GO, immediately and all at once, this new WAY he now learns about? Can any man, all at once, break all HABITS he now sees are wrong? No, he finds he has a FIGHT against acquired former habits.

He still has this PULL of this invisible but powerful Satan to overcome. This pull has been subtilely instilled as A LAW working within him—produced by the broadcasting of Satan the devil—the prince of the power of the air (Ephesians 2:2). This whole world is in tune with the very mind of the devil (Revelation 12:9).

The Apostle Paul calls this pull of human nature the law of sin and death.

Paul was *converted*. Paul was a real Christian. He had repented, accepted Christ, and received the Holy Spirit. With his MIND, he wanted with all his heart, and in real intense sincerity, to DO God's WAY! But did Paul DO it perfectly?

Let him tell. LISTEN!

PAUL'S EXPERIENCE

"For we know that the law is spiritual," he wrote, "but *I* am carnal, sold under sin. For that which I do I allow not: for what I would, that do I not; but what I hate, that do I. ... Now then it is no more I that do it, but sin that dwelleth in me." He is speaking of human nature within him. He continues, "... for to WILL is present with me; but how to perform that which is good I find not. For the good that I would I do not: but the evil which I would not, that I do. ... For I delight in the law of God after the inward man: But I *see another law* in my members, *warring against* the law of my mind, and bringing me into captivity to the law of sin which is in my members" (Romans 7:14-23).

The law of his mind is the law of God—the Ten Commandments. The law "in his members" is *human nature instilled by Satan.* Then Paul cries out, "O wretched man that I am! who shall deliver me from the body of this death?" (verse 24). Then he thanks God—that GOD WILL—through Jesus Christ, and by the power of His HOLY SPIRIT. BUT IT TAKES TIME!

The truly converted Christian will find that he often stumbles, *under temptation,* and falls down—even as a physical child learning to walk often falls down. But the year-old child does not get discouraged and give up. He gets up and starts out again.

THE TRULY CONVERTED CHRISTIAN IS NOT YET PERFECT!

GOD LOOKS ON THE HEART—the inner MOTIVE—the real *intent!* If he is trying—if he gets up whenever he falls down, and in repentance asks God's forgiveness, and sets out to do his very best NOT TO MAKE THAT MISTAKE AGAIN—and to persevere with renewed effort to OVERCOME, God is rich in mercy toward that man in his striving to overcome.

I think it should be apparent by now that the newly converted Christian is not PERFECT all at once. He does not—must not—commit sin deliberately and willfully in a spirit and attitude of rebellion. That's what he has repented of! He *wants* to live completely above sin. But to live perfectly would require all spiritual KNOWLEDGE. He would have to live by EVERY WORD of the Bible. The Holy Spirit imparts spiritual perception so he can UNDERSTAND the Bible. And to understand *all* the Bible TAKES TIME. We have to GROW into the KNOWLEDGE of HOW to live perfectly without sin.

A Christian may, from force of habit, or under weakness and temptation, sin. But if he is a Christian, he is immediately repentant, and on this repentance Christ's sacrifice cleanses his sin (1 John 1:7-9).

Converted people often are under heavier temptation than before conversion. Satan exerts more pull than before. They are STRIVING against sin, STRIVING to overcome. But they are not yet perfect. Sometimes they are caught off guard. They may actually sin. Then they WAKE UP, as it were, and realize what they have done. They REPENT. They are filled with remorse— *truly sorry*—disgusted with themselves. They go to GOD, and CRY OUT for HELP—for more power and strength from God to OVERCOME (Hebrews 4:16).

This is the WAY of the Christian!

It is the way of a constant BATTLE—a striving against SIN—a seeking God in earnest prayer for help and spiritual POWER to overcome. And if they are diligent, they are constantly GAINING GROUND. They are constantly GROWING in God's KNOWLEDGE, from the BIBLE. They are constantly rooting out wrong habits, driving themselves into RIGHT habits. They are constantly growing closer to GOD through Bible study and prayer. They are constantly growing in CHARACTER, toward perfection, even though not yet perfect.

WHAT IF ONE DIES?

But, someone may ask, what if one's life is cut off, and he dies *before* he has attained this perfection? Is he saved, or lost? The answer is that we shall never obtain absolute perfection in *this* life.

I said, earlier, that a person who is converted does receive the Holy Spirit at *a definite time*—all at once! Not the full measure Christ had—he is not at once full grown spiritually—only a spiritual babe in Christ. Yet he is then a changed, converted person—changed in mind, in attitude, in the *direction* he has set himself to travel. Even though he has not yet reached perfection—even though he may have stumbled under temptation, and taken a spiritual fall—as long as, in his mind and heart, he is earnestly striving to travel GOD'S WAY, to overcome and grow spiritually—as long as God's Spirit is in him—as long as he is being LED BY the Spirit of God, he is a begotten SON OF GOD.

If, anywhere along this life's journey, that life is cut short, such a man will be resurrected—saved—immortal in God's Kingdom.

NEVER GIVE UP AND QUIT

It is only the one who QUITS and GIVES UP (Hebrews 10:38)—who REJECTS God, and God's WAY, and rejects Christ as his Savior—who neglects or turns FROM this direction of GOD'S WAY, *in his mind and heart* (in his inner INTENT)—who deliberately and intentionally in his mind—or, from *continued* neglect—TURNS FROM Christ—who is lost.

If, once having been converted, having received God's Spirit, and TASTED of the joys of GOD'S WAY, one deliberately rejects that way, makes the DECISION, not under stress of temptation, but *deliberately* and *finally*, NOT to go God's way, then God says it is IMPOSSIBLE to renew such a one to repentance. He would have to REPENT of that decision. But if he WILLFULLY made it, not in a time of temptation, but calmly, deliberately, willfully, then he just WILL NOT ever repent of it.

But anyone who FEARS he may have committed the "unpardonable sin"—is perhaps worried about it, and HOPES he *has not* committed it, and still WANTS to have God's salvation—no such individual has committed it—such a one MAY repent, and go right on to salvation IF HE WANTS TO!

WHAT TO DO?

If you see a Christian do something wrong, DON'T SIT IN JUDGMENT AND CONDEMN—that's God's business to judge, not yours! Let's have compassion and mercy—WE don't know the inner heart of others—only GOD does!

And if you, yourself, have stumbled and fallen down, DON'T BE DISCOURAGED! Get up and press on ahead!

God looks on the heart—the attitude—the *intent*.

As long as one, in his heart, has the real desire to walk God's WAY with Him—is deeply sorry and repents when he commits the occasional sin—and is seeking to overcome sin, and to make God's way his habitual way of life, he will stumble on occasion, but if he confesses it and repents, he will be forgiven. But, if he is diligent in his Christian life, his occasional stumbling will become less and less—he will be making good progress, overcoming, GROWING spiritually and in righteous godly character.

What is your attitude? When you have sinned, have you been carelessly indifferent about it? You are on dangerous ground. Do you justify it, feel *others* are to blame? That will never *justify* your sins. Do you still *desire* to go God's way? Then it's not too late. Turn from sins, CONFESS your sins—to God. REPENT! Pick yourself up, with Christ's helping hand, and go on overcoming and GROWING spiritually.

But remember, once you know you have really repented and been forgiven, don't repeat the sin(s), but FORGET it. As the Apostle Paul wrote, "[F]ORGETTING those things which are behind, and reaching forth unto those things which are before, I press toward the mark for the prize of the high calling of God in Christ Jesus" (Philippians 3:13-14).

Chapter 11
Human Nature—and How a Whole World Is Deceived About Its Origin

I ONCE OVERHEARD SOMEONE SAY: "JUST LOOK AT THAT BEAUTIFUL, sweet little baby—and to think it's filled with all that evil, despicable human nature!"

But *was it?*

Think of this paradox! How can it be explained? The human mind can produce wonders. We have sent successive teams of men to walk on the moon. We have returned them safely through the Earth's atmosphere. Yet these marvelous human minds cannot solve our problems here on Earth—cannot bring the world PEACE! WHY? All the violence, war, crime, corruption, dishonesty and immorality is blamed on HUMAN NATURE.

But where did HUMAN NATURE come from? Did the Creator instill it within us from creation? Were we born with it? And please understand that I am speaking of human nature in its evil spiritual phase—of vanity, lust, greed, envy, jealousy, competition, strife, rebellion against authority, resentment and hate.

The answer requires a knowledge of the composition and nature of the human mind—accessible only by revelation. The composition of the human mind, as compared to animal brain, has been explained. BUT WHY does such wonderful MIND-power work so much evil?

Did an all-loving, all-merciful, Almighty GOD deliberately plague the human race He created with an inborn nature of vanity, lust and greed—with a heart of hostility against God, of deceit, envy, jealousy and hatred?

HOW WAS ADAM, AT HIS CREATION?

First, let's see what is revealed about the first man, Adam, and his nature *at the time of his creation.*

The Bible reveals only the most brief high points of human history for the first 2,000-plus years—a third of all the time from the creation of man to now! Only 11 chapters are devoted to the history of all that span of time. The account of the first created couple is merely the briefest possible summary.

The first humans were the last act of creation on the sixth day of what is commonly called "creation week," recorded in the first chapter of Genesis.

God had created plant life—the flora—on the third day of that week, animal life—the fauna—on the fifth and sixth, each reproducing *"after its own kind."* Cattle reproduced after the cattle kind (verse 25), lions after the lion kind, horses after the horse kind, etc.

Then God said, "Let us make man in our image, after our likeness..." (verse 26). In other words, "Let us make MAN *after the GOD kind!"* God was actually *reproducing Himself!*

And notice, the name God—the Hebrew name as originally written throughout Genesis 1—is *Elohim.* It is a noun or name, plural in form, like family, group, church. It is ONE family composed of more than one person. It is like one team, one church, but each composed of multiple persons. The God to whom Jesus prayed is the FATHER of the FAMILY that is GOD. God *IS* a FAMILY—but ONE family, *ONE* GOD.

"So God created man in his own image, in the image of God created he him; male and female created he them" (verse 27). WHY? Because human reproduction is the type of God's reproducing Himself. And physical reproduction requires both male and female.

But continue: "And God blessed them...." Did He *bless* them by creating in them an evil sinful nature, utterly unable to be subject to God's *right* way of life? But continue this passage: "…and God said unto them, Be fruitful, and multiply, and replenish the earth…" (verse 28).

"And God saw every thing that he had made, and, behold, it was very good" (verse 31). If the first humans—as God had created them—were VERY GOOD, could it include a hostile and evil nature that was very EVIL?

That ought to give every reader something to think about!

Now what does this record of the creation of the first humans reveal as to Adam's nature *at the time of his creation?* I repeat: Only the very most brief high spots are recorded here. The little that is revealed gives us, however, all we really need to know.

Here it is: "And out of the ground the [Eternal] God formed every beast of the field, and every fowl of the air; and brought them unto Adam to see what he would call them…" (Genesis 2:19).

Here, in the briefest of summaries, we may see clearly whether this short account reveals a rebellious and disobedient nature in Adam, or one of compliance and obedience.

Absolutely NO REBELLION is indicated here. We find, instead, the response that Adam gave names to all cattle, to the fowl of the air, and to every beast of the field.

This incident reveals Adam's attitude and nature *as he was created*, PRIOR TO his temptation by Satan (which is recorded in chapter 3). Notice carefully. Absolutely NOTHING in the account of this pre-temptation incident indicates in Adam the presence of an evil, hostile, rebellious attitude or nature. It does not reflect a heart that is deceitful above all things and desperately wicked, as human nature is described (Jeremiah 17:9), nor a carnal mind that is enmity (hostile) against God and which "is not subject to the law of God, neither indeed can be" (Romans 8:7).

Nor, on the other hand, does it reveal a nature filled with the Spirit of God. Adam had not yet been confronted by Satan, had not disobeyed, nor had he taken of the "tree of life" to receive the indwelling LOVE and POWER of God's Holy Spirit, which would have imparted the DIVINE NATURE (2 Peter 1:4).

So prior to the temptation by Satan, we have only the revelation that Adam's NATURE, as God created him, was *not* evil, hostile and diabolical. There may have been the physical and mental nature of self-preservation and such things. But *NOT* the evil nature of SELF-centeredness.

We need to realize that God created Adam and the human race for a PURPOSE. We need to have clearly in mind, at this point, WHAT that purpose is.

Angels had inhabited this planet before the creation of man (2 Peter 2:4-6). These angels had *sinned*. God had set over them a king—Lucifer, a super archangel—to govern them with the GOVERNMENT OF GOD (Isaiah 14:12-15; Ezekiel 28:11-17). All this has been covered in detail in previous chapters.

This super king, Lucifer, was, of all created beings, supreme in created perfection (Ezekiel 28:12, 15). But, remember, holy and righteous CHARACTER is something that *cannot* be created in a person *instantaneously by fiat*. It must be *developed* in an independent entity through a process in which one comes to recognize the right way from the wrong, to *choose* the right and reject the wrong even against self-desire.

The great Lucifer and the angels who followed him (apparently a third of all angels) were originally created as spirit-composed beings, immortal. But in order that they have personality and individuality as independent beings, it was necessary that they be provided with faculties for knowing, thinking, reasoning, and making their own decisions and choices.

These angels followed their king Lucifer in the decision to turn *from* and rebel *against* the GOVERNMENT OF God—God's WAY OF LIFE. That is THE WAY of *LOVE*—outgoing concern for the good of others—the way of humility, obedience to and love for their MAKER, of giving, serving, cooperating and sharing. They turned to THE WAY of vanity, lust and greed, of rebellion, jealousy, and envy, of competition, strife and violence, of resentment, bitterness and destruction. Obviously the other two thirds of the angels and archangels have remained holy, loyal, and obedient to GOD's government.

But now, to carry out God's PURPOSE for the inhabitants of this Earth, to accomplish the grand and awesome PURPOSE throughout the entire universe that could have been Lucifer's and his angels, GOD IS REPRODUCING HIMSELF THROUGH HUMAN BEINGS!

The super-archangel Lucifer was the supreme pinnacle of God's creative power in a created being. When he turned to rebellion, it left ONLY GOD Himself who could be utterly relied on NEVER to deviate from God's WAY—God's GOVERNMENT. It is impossible for God to sin—because He WILL NOT! It now became God's purpose to reproduce Himself through human beings.

That required *the development* in human beings of God's own holy, righteous CHARACTER. It was necessary, for this purpose, that man be composed of physical matter, that he CHOOSE God's government, reject Lucifer's (now Satan's) self-centered rebellious way, and strive to overcome it. God's PURPOSE in having put humans on Earth can be achieved only by man coming to choose God's GOVERNMENT as God's way of life—to reject with utter finality Satan's way, completely overcoming it.

So God created MAN out of physical matter. God created in man a MIND like God's, though of course inferior, because it was composed of physical brain, empowered with intellect by a spirit (essence) in each.

Although the holy and righteous CHARACTER to be developed within man must actually come from God, each human must make his own decision. He must make his own choice to reject Satan's WAY, strive against it, and to obey God's GOVERNMENT.

Adam was compelled, therefore, to make the choice. God purposely allowed Satan opportunity to confront Adam with his way of rebellion. But He did NOT allow Satan to get to Adam *first*. God Himself instructed Adam in GOD'S WAY—the way of the GOVERNMENT OF GOD based on the LAW OF GOD, just as Lucifer and his angels had been first instructed in the ways of THE GOVERNMENT OF GOD.

Then God allowed Satan to confront Adam. Satan got to Adam through his wife. Satan subtilely deceived Eve into DISBELIEVING what God had taught them. Adam followed her in choosing rebellion and rejecting God's rule and government over them. They took *to themselves* the knowledge of what is good and what is evil—deciding for themselves right from wrong.

Then, something happened to the minds of Adam and Eve—the eyes of both of them were opened (Genesis 3:7). The spirit and attitude of rebellion had entered their minds. Their minds (hearts) now had become perverted—deceitful and desperately wicked.

And THAT EVIL IN THEM CAME FROM SATAN, *NOT* FROM GOD! They were NOT created with this evil nature.

But how did humanity, today, come to have this evil attitude we call "HUMAN NATURE"? Did the children of Adam and Eve inherit it from them? Or, was it passed on by heredity?

Let me give you an example of heredity. God put Adam to sleep and removed one of his ribs, out of which He made Eve. Do all men today find themselves short one rib by heredity? Of course not. *Acquired* characteristics *are not passed on by heredity.*

Adam and Eve chose *and acquired* the "nature" or attitude of sin from Satan. It was not passed on by heredity. Jesus Christ called their second son "righteous Abel."

Then how *do* we humans come to have (universally) this evil attitude we call human nature today?

It's partly explained in the Apostle Paul's second letter to the Corinthian church. He said he desired to present that church "as a chaste virgin to Christ. BUT I fear, lest by any means, *as the serpent beguiled Eve* through his subtilty, *so* your minds should be corrupted from the simplicity that is in Christ" (2 Corinthians 11:2-3).

Satan was still around when Paul wrote. (The reason is explained elsewhere.) The people at Corinth had not received this evil nature *by heredity.* Rather, the apostle feared lest they (in this NEW Testament time) should be beguiled into evil attitudes *in the same manner* as was the original mother Eve— directly by Satan.

Eve did not have a mind that was evil *before* Satan came along and confronted her. But Satan, by subtileness, deceived Eve. Eve's children were not born with this evil nature. Nor were the people of the Corinthian church. But Paul feared lest Satan, still around after some 4,000 years, pervert Corinthian minds directly, *as* he had done to Eve.

Satan was still around when Christ was born. He tried to destroy the Christ-child by having Him murdered. Satan was still around when Jesus was 30 and baptized. And he tried to destroy Jesus spiritually then, in the temptation. As Satan destroyed (spiritually) Adam, he tried to destroy the "second Adam." Satan is still around TODAY!

But the wily Satan has succeeded in deluding many, if not most, of the best minds into believing he is a nonexistent myth. The best minds, unsuspecting, are deceived (Revelation 12:9).

Here is a TRUTH you, the reader, NEED TO KNOW!

To the Church at Ephesus, God said through the Apostle Paul: "And you [who] … in time past … walked according to the course of this world, *according to the prince of the power of the air,* the spirit *that now worketh in* the children of disobedience" (Ephesians 2:1-2).

GRASP IT! Satan is here called *"the prince of the power of the AIR"*! I could not have understood that 60 years ago. I did not then realize how communication by sound and by picture can be broadcast instantaneously *through the air.*

In past chapters I have stressed the point that Satan, the former great archangel cherub Lucifer, was the most perfect and powerful being that God could create as an individual being. He was perfect as originally created. But he is composed of spirit, and thus he is invisible to human eyes.

This great and powerful being, even though evil, has power literally to surcharge the air around this Earth. HE BROADCASTS!

Wherever you are as you read these words, chances are there are voices and perhaps music *in the air* around you. A radio or TV set tuned to the right wavelength would make them audible and visible to you.

The spirit in every human being is automatically tuned in on Satan's wavelength. You don't hear anything because he does not broadcast in words—nor in sounds, whether music or otherwise. He broadcasts in ATTITUDES. He broadcasts in attitudes of SELF-centeredness, lust, greed, vanity, jealousy, envy, resentment, competition, strife, bitterness and hate.

In a word, the selfishness, hostility, deceitfulness, wickedness, rebellion, etc. that we call "HUMAN NATURE" is actually SATAN'S NATURE. It is Satan's ATTITUDE. And broadcasting it, surcharging the air with it, Satan actually NOW WORKS *IN* the unsuspecting all over the world today! That is *HOW* Satan deceives the whole world today (Revelation 12:9; 20:3). Being invisible, people do not see or hear him.

This prince of the power of the air—this god of this world—IS THE REAL SOURCE OF WHAT WE HAVE COME TO CALL "HUMAN NATURE"!

Here is the real CAUSE of all the world's evils!

But it seems *nobody* understands it, and therefore the world does nothing about it—except to go along with it blaming human nature and supposing it was God who created us with an evil nature when actually it is Satan's.

Let me give you an illustration of how we can be swayed, influenced and driven by Satan's broadcasting through the air. When God wanted to cause captive Jews in ancient Babylon to return to Jerusalem to build the second temple, He put it in the mind of Cyrus, king of Persia. The Persian Empire had taken over the rule of empire from Babylon. Following is the explanation of how God moved Cyrus to do what God wanted.

"Now in the first year of Cyrus king of Persia ... the [Eternal] stirred up the spirit of Cyrus king of Persia, that he made a proclamation throughout all his kingdom ..." (Ezra 1:1) that a contingent of Jews return to Jerusalem.

God did not speak to Cyrus in words or direct communication, as He talked with Moses and God's prophets. God reached Cyrus *through Cyrus's spirit*. God stirred up his spirit, causing him to want to do it. God did cause King Cyrus to know that in issuing this proclamation he was doing it according to the will of God.

Utilizing this same principle, Satan, prince of THE POWER OF THE AIR, stirs the spirits of humans, injecting into them attitudes, moods, and impulses of selfishness, vanity, lust and greed, attitudes of resentment against authority, of jealousy and envy, of competition and strife, of resentment and bitterness, of violence, murder and war. People do not recognize the source of these attitudes, feelings, motives and impulses. As I said, they do not SEE the invisible Satan. They hear no audible voice. They do not know the attitude came from Satan (Revelation 12:9). But they come to FEEL such attitudes, impulses and desires. That is how Satan DECEIVES THE WHOLE WORLD.

People will feel depressed and won't realize why. But those unaware of this phenomenon, with this self-centered attitude being broadcast and injected into their unsuspecting minds from earliest childhood, do, to a greater or lesser degree, absorb it until it becomes their normal attitude. It becomes habitual. It does not, of course, exhibit the *same degree* of effect in all minds—one person will become more evil than another. But the natural tendency is there. They come to have it *naturally*. It becomes their very NATURE. And we call it "human nature."

All this is an outstanding example of just *how subtle* Satan is! The finest and most brilliant human minds have been deceived by it. Thus the WHOLE WORLD has been swayed by Satan into what I often term, simply, the "GET" way of life—the way that has become HABITUAL and NATURAL which we term "HUMAN NATURE."

Few realize how many passages in the Bible, especially in the New Testament, warn us about Satan and his subtileness. But first, before I take you to more of these, let us follow on through this second chapter of Ephesians.

In chapter 1 of this letter to the Church at Ephesus, the Apostle Paul gives thanks and praise to God who has blessed "us" (the converts at Ephesus *and* Paul—also all Christians) with every spiritual blessing within the heavenly sphere. God had chosen us before we were born—before the foundation of the world—being predestined to be called to spiritual salvation. God has richly *lavished* on us His grace. He shows that we being called in this time—this New Testament "church age"—are the *first* to be called to this glorious grace (emphasizing that this is NOT the time God is trying to save all the world, but only those predestined to be called NOW). Paul had heard of their faith and prayed for their eyes to be opened fully to the awesome human potential—the supreme greatness of their divine heritage.

I urgently suggest the reader carefully read this first chapter in the Moffatt translation. As translated by Moffatt I think it is one of the most beautiful, uplifting and inspiring pieces of literature I have ever read.

Now the highlights of chapter 2: You Christians at Ephesus were spiritually dead, but Christ has given you the impregnation of eternal life. You are now spiritually alive. In the past you lived according to the way of this world (the SELF-centered way), according to the PRINCE OF THE POWER OF THE AIR. In 2 Corinthians 4:4 Satan is called the god of this world, who has blinded the minds of those who do not believe in Christ and His truth. NOT that they inherited this spiritual blindness—but that *Satan* blinded those living in that generation *directly.*

And in Ephesians 2 Satan is referred to as the PRINCE OF THE POWER OF THE AIR. Notice the word *POWER*—the POWER of the air! Then it calls him the SPIRIT (being) that NOW—the time when they were living—actually was WORKING IN those of the world who were not obedient—that is, the world in general. The Phillips translation in modern English renders this: "You [then] drifted along in the stream of this world's ideas of living, and obeyed its unseen ruler [who is still operating in those who do not respond to the truth of God]."

Emphatically this shows Satan is the UNSEEN one who, unrealized by the people, is actually swaying their minds, leading them in what I term the "GET" way.

The Phillips translation continues (verse 3): "We all lived like that in the past, and followed the impulses and imaginations of our evil nature … like everyone else." This "nature" has been *acquired* from Satan. It was not inherited from our parents. It was not created in us by God. That which has become *habitual* and therefore *natural* becomes a NATURE within us.

Such nature IS NOT hereditary, but an *acquired* characteristic. This very passage shows the AUTHOR of this "nature" to be Satan, NOT GOD. The next words in the Phillips translation are: "being under the wrath of God by nature." It would make no sense at all for God's wrath to be on us BECAUSE OF WHAT GOD PUTS WITHIN US. Adam was NOT created with this "EVIL nature." Adam acquired it from Satan. Lucifer (Satan) was created PERFECT. He acquired it by false reasoning. These Ephesians, in their generation, had acquired it from Satan. But now, IN CHRIST, through His grace, Christ had given them LIFE, who *were* spiritually dead because of this acquired evil nature.

But how about the converted Christian? His spirit (mind), like all others, is tuned on Satan's wavelength. The same tendency, just as if this evil nature were inherent in him from birth, is present. Satan has been injecting it since early childhood. But the true Christian has repented of that WAY. He has REJECTED it. He has turned from it. He has accepted and turned *to* GOD's way—the way of GOD's GOVERNMENT!

The passage in Ephesians 2 explains it. People generally, in the world, are spiritually dead. They have gone along with the rest of the world in the self-centered way. As the Phillips translation renders it, they have "drifted along on the stream of this world's way of living." They have "obeyed its UNSEEN ruler [who is still operating in those who do not respond to the truth of God]."

I have quoted from the Phillips translation, not because it is a more accurate or dependable translation, but because it brought out the meaning more clearly in this particular passage.

Conversion *does not disconnect* Satan's wavelength. The tendency to become resentful over real or fancied wrongs or injustices from others, the tendency to try to get the best of others, may still prove a temptation. THESE are the things the converted Christian must strive *to overcome!*

When Jesus spoke of OVERCOMING, He referred to overcoming these WAYS of Satan, which are contrary to GOD's way. The Christian must, as Peter was inspired to write, GROW in grace and in the KNOWLEDGE of our Lord and Savior Jesus Christ.

We read in James 4: "Submit yourselves therefore to God. Resist the devil, and he will flee from you" (verse 7). This is speaking of resisting these very self-centered thoughts, attitudes, tendencies and ways which Satan injected into us from childhood and is constantly broadcasting and injecting into unsuspecting minds through the spirit in man.

However, no man is IMPELLED to respond to and obey these impulses being broadcast by Satan. Satan has no power of duress to FORCE anyone to think or do wrong. But the unsuspecting automatically do without fully realizing what is taking place in their minds. They "drift along."

The passage in 2 Corinthians 4:4 adds clarity to the entire thesis that this evil spiritual nature in humans has been *acquired,* individually by each person, from Satan.

Before I became familiar with radio, I could not have understood HOW Satan injects this evil attitude into humans. He is a SUPERPOWERFUL spirit being. He was set on a throne as king over the Earth. He himself, by his own reasoning processes, *acquired* this evil nature. God did not create it in him (Ezekiel 28:15). Though disqualified now to administer the GOVERNMENT OF GOD over the Earth, he must remain here *UNTIL* his successor has qualified *AND* been inducted into office. There is a REASON why Christ has not YET come to take over that office, remove Satan, and *restore* the government of God.

Before Jesus Christ could qualify to restore the GOVERNMENT OF GOD and RULE all nations, He had to withstand Satan's most severe temptation. You'll read of that supreme struggle in the fourth chapter of Matthew. Jesus had to—*in human flesh*—reject Satan's way and teach and prove OBEDIENT to the GOVERN-MENT OF GOD—so He can RESTORE it on Earth!

It was immediately after that—after Christ QUALIFIED to restore the GOVERNMENT OF GOD to Earth—that Jesus came into Galilee, preaching the gospel of the KINGDOM OF GOD, and saying, "The time is fulfilled…" (Mark 1:1, 14-15). It was never fulfilled until that titanic struggle in which Jesus resisted Satan, conquered him, and showed His MASTERY over him.

Now notice something you probably never realized before:

I have said repeatedly THIS IS *NOT* THE TIME GOD IS TRYING TO CONVERT THE WHOLE WORLD. He is calling only a comparative *VERY FEW*, now.

WHY? WHY does not God call everyone on Earth *NOW?*

Are those of us called NOW getting a real SPECIAL deal?

Well, THINK OF THIS: We, now called, *must resist Satan,* who will PULL OUT ALL STOPS to attack and DESTROY those of us called NOW!

All others are drifting along SATAN'S WAY *ANYWAY*. Sure, he broadcasts to sway *everyone* to his SELF-centered way, contrary to GOD'S WAY. But he has the whole world already going his way. But those of us who have turned from his way, are fighting to OVERCOME his way, and turning to GOD'S way—the WAY of God's GOVERNMENT—are the ones Satan HATES. He seeks specially to destroy us! Without God's protection and restraining power over Satan, we could never make it!

Few, even among professing converted Christians, realize the vital and SUPREME NEED to be conscious and constantly aware of Satan's efforts to get to US, who already have turned *from* Satan's way and *to* the WAY of the GOVERNMENT OF GOD. For this very reason, Satan has gotten to and overthrown many who have fallen away (2 Thessalonians 2:3).

Few actively heed what God, through Paul, said later to the Ephesians: "Finally, my brethren, be strong in the Lord, and in the power of his might. Put on the whole armour of God, that ye may be able to stand against the wiles of the devil. For we wrestle not against flesh and blood, but against principali-ties, against POWERS, against the rulers of the darkness of this world, against spiritual wickedness [wicked SPIRITS] in HIGH PLACES" (Ephesians 6:10-12).

There is a reason WHY God allows those predestinated to be called NOW to have to withstand Satan and his REBELLION AGAINST THE GOVERNMENT OF GOD.

It is necessary—in order for us to QUALIFY to become rulers (under Christ) in the KINGDOM OF GOD—that we NOT ONLY reject Satan's false way but *strive against* it until we OVERCOME IT, relying all the while on GOD for the power to do so.

As we, from earliest childhood growing up, *acquired* Satan's nature, so, through conversion and the struggle of OVERCOMING, we rid ourselves of it. We ACQUIRE, instead, the DIVINE NATURE. Peter wrote that we become "PARTAKERS OF THE DIVINE NATURE" (2 Peter 1:4). We most certainly were not born with it.

So, Lucifer ACQUIRED that "satanic" nature by his own reasoning and choice. Humans have ACQUIRED Satan's nature from childhood and call it "human nature." But converted Christians, who reject Satan's way and OVERCOME it, turning to GOD'S WAY, BECOME PARTAKERS OF—i.e., ACQUIRE—the DIVINE NATURE. But for God's PURPOSE, it was necessary that we first know and totally REJECT Satan's way and accept GOD'S GOVERNMENT.

When God does set out to CALL EVERY HUMAN ON EARTH to spiritual salvation, Satan will be BOUND a thousand years, unable to broadcast his impulses and attitudes. The world will be at *PEACE!* Those called then will not have to battle what we do now.

But *WHY?* There has to be a REASON!

To those of us being called, NOW, Jesus said: "And he that overcometh [Satan and his own self], and keepeth my works unto the end, to him will I give power over the nations: And he shall rule them with a rod of iron ..." (Revelation 2:26-27).

When Christ comes to RULE, as the KING of kings and LORD of lords, we who are called now will rule with and under Him, as He restores the GOVERNMENT OF GOD to this Earth.

Notice again: "To him that overcometh will I grant to sit with me in my throne, even as I also overcame, and am set down with my Father in his throne" (Revelation 3:21). Those who shall reign WITH Christ, when He comes to restore the GOVERNMENT OF GOD, MUST OVERCOME (and that includes overcoming SATAN), EVEN AS JESUS DID!

Now does this apply equally to those who shall be converted *after* Christ comes, during the Millennium?

The answer is *NO!* These two quotations (above) are found in Jesus's message to the seven CHURCHES that span this CHURCH AGE! They do NOT apply to those called later! Do they apply *only* to the era of Thyatira and Laodicea? No, they apply to ALL the Church age. These seven messages DO apply to *seven successive Church eras.* BUT they *also* apply to the WHOLE CHURCH through ALL eras. In other words, the Ephesus characteristics DOMINATED in the first era, and the Laodicean will dominate in the last, but SOME of these characteristics are found in EVERY era. The messages apply to the WHOLE Church (and so I have said and written for more than 50 years), but certain characteristics predominate in the various eras.

But GET THIS CRUX POINT! Jesus had to QUALIFY to RULE the Earth. God's WHOLE PURPOSE IS TO RESTORE THE GOVERNMENT of GOD on Earth and set up the KINGDOM OF GOD. Jesus had to resist and overcome the temptations—very special ones—of SATAN. Are WE to rule *without* any such qualifications? *Of course not!* Those who are to rule with and under Christ when He restores the GOVERNMENT to the Earth MUST QUALIFY—must turn FROM Satan's WAY TO GOD's WAY, that is, to the GOVERNMENT of GOD. We must root out—root and branch—Satan's ATTITUDE and WAY, and so thoroughly that we shall make it IMPOSSIBLE ever to turn again to Satan's way—IMPOSSIBLE TO SIN (1 John 3:9).

Those called to spiritual salvation AFTER Christ comes will not have to battle Satan.

Notice Matthew 25 and Revelation 20:

First, Matthew 25, beginning verse 31: "When the Son of man shall come in his glory, and all the holy angels with him, then shall he sit upon the throne of his glory." Christ is coming in all the supreme POWER and GLORY of the Creator GOD! He is coming to RESTORE THE GOVERNMENT OF GOD over the WHOLE EARTH—over ALL NATIONS! One SUPER WORLD GOVERNMENT! He will restore the throne of David at Jerusalem. Since 1968 the Ambassador International Cultural Foundation, through the auspices of the Worldwide Church of God, has been in joint participation with Hebrew University and the Israel Archaeological Society in excavations in Jerusalem, and in clearing off some 50 feet or more of debris which has covered the ancient throne of David, which existed some 2,500 years ago.

Continue: "And before him shall be gathered all nations…" (verse 32). He is coming to RULE the WORLD—to RESTORE the GOVERNMENT OF GOD!

Every government is founded on a basic LAW. The law of God is unlike any man-made law of any human government. It is a SPIRITUAL law (Romans 7:14). And it is a HOLY law (Romans 7:12). It is A WAY OF LIFE—*God's way!* When people are governed in that way of life, there will be PEACE, HAPPINESS, JOY, ABUNDANCE!

But that basic LAW of the GOVERNMENT OF GOD is also the law of the Christian WAY of life. Sin is the transgression of that law (1 John 3:4). Christ is coming also to call ALL PEOPLE to spiritual salvation and eternal life. That is when God will seek to spiritually save THE WHOLE WORLD—and NOT TILL THEN!

Continue: "[A]nd he shall separate them one from another, as a shepherd divideth his sheep from the goats: And he shall set the sheep on his right hand, but the goats on the left. Then shall the King say unto them on his right hand, Come, ye blessed of my Father, inherit the kingdom prepared for you from the foundation of the world" (Matthew 25:32-34).

The nations before the king on his throne are the nations of this world. Those called to and qualified for salvation during that Church age and previously (prophets, etc.), will have been resurrected to meet Christ in the air, as He descends to Earth on His return (1 Thessalonians 4:16-17). They will be ruling with Christ, already being immortal, composed of spirit (Revelation 2:26-27; 3:21). They, with Christ, will compose the KINGDOM OF GOD.

It is necessary, here, to explain the difference between the GOVERNMENT OF GOD and the KINGDOM OF GOD. The GOVERNMENT of God was established on Earth IN PRE-HISTORY OVER THE ANGELS.

But the KINGDOM of God is BOTH the GOVERNMENT of God and the FAMILY of God. Those now being saved spiritually will, in the resurrection, INHERIT the Kingdom of God. They shall have been BORN of God—born into the divine FAMILY of God. They shall be married to Christ. Of this divine spiritual marriage, children of God will be begotten and born spiritually all during the thousand years commencing with Christ's return to Earth as KING.

Now let's notice the 20th chapter of Revelation:

The Apostle John is recording what he saw in vision: "And I saw an angel come down from heaven, having the key of the bottomless pit and a great chain in his hand. And he laid hold on the dragon, that old serpent, which is the Devil, and Satan, and bound him a thousand years" (Revelation 20:1-2).

When Christ comes again to Earth in supreme POWER and GLORY, He shall already have been crowned with many crowns. The coronation ceremony will have taken place in heaven (the throne of God the Father) before His return. Christ then shall have been qualified *AND* inducted into office. I have said before, Satan must remain on Earth swaying the nations his way UNTIL Christ, the successor, has both qualified AND been inducted into office.

Immediately on Christ's return, Satan shall be BOUND.

Continue: "And cast him into the bottomless pit, and shut him up, and set a seal upon him, that he should deceive the nations no more, till the thousand years should be fulfilled: and after that he must be loosed a little season" (verse 3).

Those resurrected then shall reign over all nations with Christ—and a thousand years of PEACE on Earth will ensue.

Imagine what it shall be like with Christ and resurrected saints forming the KINGDOM OF GOD, ruling with the GOVERN-MENT OF GOD over all living humans who shall be left alive. Satan will be restrained from broadcasting. Christ will be ruling with GOD's WAY of life.

But NOW NOTICE! "And when the thousand years are expired, Satan shall be loosed out of his prison, And shall go out to deceive the nations which are in the four quarters of the earth ... to gather them together to battle: the number of whom is as the sand of the sea" (verses 7-8).

Grasp it! These are people at PEACE! They shall not be inoculated with the satanic NATURE we now call "human nature." They shall have been living happily in PERFECT PEACE. Now Satan once more BROADCASTS. Remember these nations are HUMAN. Satan is INVISIBLE to them. But notice the CHANGE come over them as soon as Satan is loosed and able again to sway humanity:

Verse 9: "And they [the human nations] went up on the breadth of the earth, and compassed the camp of the saints about, and the beloved city ...." Immediately "HUMAN NATURE" shall have entered into them! Immediately they shall have been filled with envy and jealousy against the saints of God, filled with wrath and violence! But God will not allow them to destroy. They shall have been *told*—have been warned about Satan. "[A]nd fire came down from God out of heaven, and devoured them. And the devil that deceived them was cast into the lake of fire and brimstone … and shall be tormented day and night for ever and ever" (verses 9-10).

After this shall occur the Great White Throne Judgment—the resurrection of *all humanity* from the time of Adam to Christ's Second Coming who had not been in the first resurrection or called by God. In this judgment is to be "the book of life," meaning many, perhaps most, shall then find spiritual salvation and eternal life. In the time of their judgment, Satan will be GONE!

Up to now, God has called VERY FEW to spiritual salvation, contrary to general tradition and opinion in the "Christian" world!

From Adam to Noah we have the record of only Abel, Enoch and Noah—some 1,900 years! From Noah to Christ, there was Abraham, Lot, Isaac, Jacob and Joseph, prior to calling the children of Israel out of Egypt. God NEVER offered spiritual salvation (eternal life) to the Old Testament nation Israel, but only to the prophets and those called to SPECIAL DUTY.

From Adam to Christ, NONE were called to spiritual salvation *except those called to perform a SPECIAL MISSION.*

From Christ to now, only a VERY MINUTE PORTION of humanity has been called, and they for the SPECIAL MISSION of THE GREAT COMMISSION—"Go ye into all the world, and preach the GOSPEL" (of the KINGDOM OF GOD).

We who have been called in this "Church age" have been called to qualify as rulers with and under Christ in the Kingdom of God, restoring the GOVERNMENT OF GOD—in other words, to develop the holy, righteous CHARACTER of God. But OUR PART in the GREAT COMMISSION is the assignment God has given as THE MEANS of preparing us for rulership with and under Christ when He comes—and THAT IS NOW SOON!

This chapter began with the question of whether this evil "human nature" is born in a sweet tiny baby. Let me now just quote three passages from the Bible.

"And they brought unto him [Jesus] also infants, that he would touch them.... Jesus called them unto him, and said, Suffer little children to come unto me, and forbid them not: for *of* such is the kingdom of God" (Luke 18:15-16). The evil nature which some erroneously have supposed was born in babies is the nature of Satan's kingdom, but "of such"—*these babies*—is the Kingdom of GOD.

"At the same time came the disciples unto Jesus, saying, Who is the greatest in the kingdom of heaven? And Jesus called a little child unto him, and set him in the midst of them, And said, Verily I say unto you, Except ye be converted, *and become as* little children, ye shall not enter into the kingdom of heaven" (Matthew 18:1-3).

"...Jesus said, Suffer *little* children, and forbid them not, to come unto me: for of such is the kingdom of heaven" (Matthew 19:14).

We humans start out at birth all right. We begin our human life with neither the "human nature" from Satan nor the divine nature which may be imparted only by the Holy Spirit. But soon we begin to absorb and ACQUIRE the selfish, self-centered attitude broadcast by Satan. But Satan's kingdom of angels—now turned to demons—rejected the GOVERNMENT OF GOD, and it was thus removed from Earth.

GOD's PURPOSE in having created and put HUMANS on Earth was to develop in them GOD's own holy and righteous character. God wants a people who will REJECT and overcome Satan's WAY OF LIFE and turn to THE GOVERNMENT OF GOD—which is GOD's WAY of life.

That GOVERNMENT OF GOD exists at this time on Earth only through those that are being led by God's Spirit within the Church of God. Satan is angry. He hates it! He subtly tries to inject into minds under that government of LOVE a hostility that MISrepresents it as a harsh and cruel government of Satan.

But I repeat, LUCIFER was created by God "*perfect* in all his ways, until iniquity was found in him." He *acquired* the nature of rebellion and evil by false reasoning. Adam *acquired* it from Satan. The Ephesians (Ephesians 2:1) *acquired it from Satan— as has all humanity, except* Jesus Christ. But now, IN CHRIST, through His grace, we may ACQUIRE the DIVINE NATURE OF GOD (2 Peter 1:4).

God's GREAT PURPOSE is to RESTORE THE GOVERNMENT OF GOD to this Earth, in and through the KINGDOM OF GOD!

We CAN, by Christ's grace, CHANGE "human nature" and eradicate it entirely from us, replacing it with the DIVINE NATURE!

Chapter 12
Is There Life After Death?

WHY THIS MYSTERY ABOUT LIFE AFTER DEATH? WHY SO MANY beliefs of so many different religions? How can we KNOW? Can we believe God? Adam and Eve didn't. Few believed Christ—that is, few believed what He SAID! Could we believe God—if He *told us?*

I said to my wife more than 50 years ago, "I know the Bible says, 'Thou shalt keep Sunday.'" "How do you know?" she asked. "Did you read it?"

"No, but I know it's there, because all these Christian churches get their religion from the Bible, and they all keep Sunday."

"Why don't you look it up and show it to me?" she challenged.

But I couldn't find it.

I chanced to read in Romans 6:23: "[T]he wages of sin is DEATH...." "Now wait a minute!" I exclaimed, surprised. "In Sunday school they taught me the wages we earn for sinning is IMMORTAL LIFE, not death—eternal life *in hell fire.*" Then I read the remainder of the verse, "...but the GIFT of God is eternal life...."

"That's a shocker!" I expressed, further surprised. "I thought I already *had* eternal life. I'm an IMMORTAL SOUL."

I had left church and Sunday school when I was 18. But I had been brought up in an established and respectable Christian denomination. I became intrigued. I had heard the preacher say, "The Bible says, when we all get to HEAVEN...." I chanced to read where Jesus said, "[N]o man hath ascended up to heaven." And after reading a few more plain biblical statements, I began to believe that even the churches TODAY *do not believe* what Jesus SAID!

Yes, more than 50 years ago my mind was *swept clean* of all previous teaching, suppositions and ideas about things relating to God. I had then *proved* the infallible inspiration of the Bible in its original writing.

I was right to believe what God says in His Word.

What *does* the Bible say about life after death? Did anyone ever die and then actually *experience* a life *after death*—and who could PROVE IT and explain to us what that life was like?

The answer is YES. Jesus Christ Himself died and was DEAD. But He rose from the dead and was seen by MANY—including His disciples, who had been with Him for 3½ years *before* He died, and 40 days *after* His resurrection. And they went about loudly proclaiming that they were eyewitnesses of His LIFE AFTER DEATH.

In 1 Corinthians 15:22-23, you will read: "For as in Adam all die, even so in Christ shall all be made alive [after death]. But every man in his own order...."

The 15th chapter of 1 Corinthians is the "resurrection chapter" of the Bible. Its subject is the resurrection to LIFE, *after death!* But there is in God's master plan an *order*—or succession—of resurrections.

Continue: "...Christ the firstfruits"—this occurred more than 1,900 years ago—"afterward they that are Christ's at his coming. Then cometh the end..." (verses 23-24).

Later in this chapter a great deal will be said about the resurrection of those "that are Christ's"—Spirit-begotten Christians. But what of the *others?*

The same ALL who die in Adam, it says, "in Christ shall... be made alive"—by a resurrection from the dead. Verse 23 says, "...they that are Christ's [shall be resurrected] at his [second] coming"—now imminent—in our present generation. "Then cometh the end" (verse 24)—but the details of the resurrection of others—the overwhelming majority of all who ever lived—are recorded elsewhere.

In Revelation 20 we find described two more resurrections. First, verse 4, the saints who are Christ's are to live and reign on the Earth with Christ for 1,000 years. Satan will be put away (verses 1-2) but the rest of those who have died will not live again until after that thousand years (verse 5). Then, beginning verse 11:

"And I saw a great white throne, and him that sat on it, from whose face the earth and the heaven fled away; and there was found no place for them. And I saw the dead, small and great, stand before God" (the second resurrection); "and the books were opened: and another book was opened, which is the book of life: and the dead were judged ... according to their works."

This will be by far the GREATEST resurrection, in numbers resurrected. It will include the BILLIONS who have lived CUT OFF from God—who were *not then* judged.

The Bible is essentially the book concerning the nation Israel. The resurrection of all of them, not previously called to spiritual salvation, is recorded in Ezekiel 37.

The Prophet Ezekiel was taken in a vision and set down in a valley filled with very dry bones. In verse 11 it is recorded that God told him that these bones were the whole house of Israel. They—these dead skeletons—were pictured saying, "Our bones are dried and our hope is lost."

But the prophet was told to say to these dry skeletons, "Thus saith the [Eternal] God, Behold, O my people, I will open your graves, and cause you to come up out of your graves, and bring you into the land of Israel."

In the vision, before God explained to the prophet the identity of the great valley of skeletons, the prophet was told to say to the dry bones, "Thus saith the [Eternal] God ... Behold, I will cause breath to enter into you, and ye shall live: And I will lay sinews upon you, and will bring up flesh upon you, and cover you with skin, and put breath in you, and ye shall live ..." (verses 5-6). Now back to verse 13: "And ye shall know that I am the [Eternal], when I have opened your graves, O my people, and brought you up out of your graves. And shall put my spirit in you, and ye shall live, and I shall place you in your own land: then shall ye know that I the [Eternal] have spoken it, and performed it, saith the [Eternal]."

This prophecy is of a resurrection to mortal flesh-and-blood life—not a resurrection, like that of the saints at Christ's Second Coming, to immortal spirit-composed self-existent life.

God had never offered Old Testament Israel His Spirit, or spiritual salvation. Only material and national promises—and even that for obedience which they refused to give.

But now, in this Great White Throne resurrection, along with all other peoples who had been CUT OFF from God, these Israelites (including those who were uncalled even after Christ came), would be resurrected to mortal, breathing, flesh-and-blood life. They all, hopefully, are then to come to really KNOW that the Eternal is Lord, and He shall, upon their eventual conversion, put His Holy Spirit within them. They, too—along with all of every nation, who had not been specially called prior to the Millennium—shall live again physically in this resurrection. And after a period of growth and overcoming, then shall come their spiritual salvation—with no Satan around to deceive them!

Now back to Revelation 20. Verses 13 to 15 indicate that there will then be a last, final resurrection of the incorrigible who have rejected the eternal salvation offered them. They, with any such living at the end of the Millennium, will then die the *second death*—utter extinction—in the lake of fire, described by Peter as the face of the Earth becoming a molten mass.

Malachi adds: "For, behold, the day cometh, that shall burn as an oven; and all the proud, yea, and all that do wickedly, shall be stubble: and the day that cometh shall *burn them up,* saith the [Eternal] of hosts, that it shall leave them neither root nor branch. But unto you that fear my name shall the Sun of righteousness arise with healing in his wings; and ye shall go forth…. And ye shall tread down the wicked; for *they shall be ashes under the soles of your feet* in the day that I shall do this, saith the [Eternal] of hosts" (Malachi 4:1-3). "[A]nd they shall be as though they had not been" (Obadiah 16).

But, what, in the meantime—what between the second of one's death and the resurrection? The Bible teaching, contrary to much religious and church teaching—that is the WORD OF GOD teaching—is that the dead ARE DEAD—utterly unconscious.

Notice the inspired wisdom of Solomon: "For the living know that they shall die: but the dead know not any thing…"—the RSV translates it, "the dead KNOW NOTHING" (Ecclesiastes 9:5).

One of God's ministers told me of experiences he has had with three successive would-be suicides. Each time he said to them, "Well, go right ahead—but first you'd better learn what happens at the moment you die. So far as your consciousness goes, the next fraction of a second you will wake up in the resurrection—and if you commit this self-murder, you'll *still* be facing all your problems, and the guilt of this SELF-MURDER crime in addition. Why not solve the problems NOW, before you commit this murder?" Not one of the three went on through with his intended suicide!

So, there's nothing to gain by "ending it all," thinking that is the *easy* way out. Death only brings *instant* awakening in the resurrection. You will know absolutely NOTHING from the second you die till the second you awake in the resurrection. These men, the minister explained, had supposed that suicide would END IT ALL—and they'd be out of their troubles, but when they learned they would still have their troubles plus a MURDER charge against them in THAT JUDGEMENT, it no longer seemed that suicide was the "quick way out of it all."

No, death is not a friend, but an ENEMY! Christ came to DESTROY DEATH—to make a happy, peaceful, abundant life possible for all—for each in his own due time. He came that we might have LIFE, "and have it more abundantly."

There most certainly is life after death—and Christ made possible a transcendent human potential so great it seems incredible. He came to DIE in our stead—to pay the penalty we have incurred *for us,* and to GIVE US LIFE!

Christ Himself taught that there is LIFE AFTER DEATH.

He taught the Pharisee Nicodemus, but Nicodemus didn't believe Him! Jesus said to him, "…I have told you earthly things, and ye believe not…" (John 3:12).

Why didn't the Pharisee Nicodemus understand when Jesus said to him: "Except a man be born again, he cannot see the kingdom of God"? (verse 3).

Why do people not understand those words today? How many know, today, that Jesus's gospel was a sensational, never-before-proclaimed NEWS ANNOUNCEMENT?

JESUS WAS A NEWSCASTER

Those in Judea knew—or should have known—Malachi's prophecy concerning this. It was the gospel of God—and the word "gospel" means GOOD NEWS!

Jesus was a NEWSCASTER. His news was something absolutely NEW—never before proclaimed to mankind. It was the most wonderful NEWS ever reported, actually almost too wonderful for humans to believe. It was news of the utterly transcendent potential of man.

The tremendous message that Jesus brought was not a report of past events. It was ADVANCE news of an almost unbelievable UTOPIAN WORLD TOMORROW! It was news of life after death. And it was news that we may be BORN AGAIN! Yet almost nobody understands it!

Why has it never been recognized by the world as the stupendous NEWS that it actually was?

Because first-century enemies of the gospel SUPPRESSED IT!

The Church of God, on the foundation of the original apostles and Christ, was founded on the day of Pentecost, A.D. 31. About two decades later, when the Apostle Paul wrote his letter to the churches of Galatia, it had already been suppressed, and false ministers had turned the people to a DIFFERENT GOSPEL. Paul wrote, "I marvel that ye are so soon removed from him that called you into the grace of Christ unto *another gospel:* Which is not another; but there be some that trouble you, and *would pervert the gospel of Christ*" (Galatians 1:6-7). Again, in Romans 1:18: "For the wrath of God is revealed from heaven against all ungodliness and wickedness of men who by their wickedness *suppress the truth*" (RSV). And in 2 Corinthians 11 Paul speaks of false apostles of Satan (verses 13-15) who *come preaching* "another gospel" (verses 4, 13, 15).

The time was at hand, when Jesus preached, for this message to be announced! The time is at hand, today, for its true MEANING to be made so PLAIN that people may UNDERSTAND IT! (Matthew 24:14).

It WILL BE, in this chapter. And it is a crucial CHALLENGE to you who now read it! And you have to UNDERSTAND what was that news announcement, or you can never UNDERSTAND what Jesus meant about being "born again."

WHAT WAS THE NEWS?

Notice, briefly, first, what that astonishing NEWS message was! The preannouncement, in Malachi's prophecy, says: "Behold,

I will send my messenger, and he shall prepare the way before me: and the Lord, whom ye seek [the Messiah], shall suddenly come to his temple, even the messenger of the covenant..." (Malachi 3:1).

Now notice the beginning of the MESSENGER's proclamation of the MESSAGE. It is recorded in Mark's gospel, chapter 1: "The beginning of the gospel of Jesus Christ, the Son of God; As it is written in the prophets...." Then follows the citation from Malachi, written above. That is followed by the account of John the Baptist, preparing the way before the Messenger.

Then, verses 14-15: "Now after that John was put in prison, Jesus came into Galilee, preaching the gospel of the kingdom of God, And saying, The time is fulfilled, and the kingdom of God is at hand: repent ye, and believe the gospel"—that is, BELIEVE the good news!

WHAT IS THE KINGDOM OF GOD?

What did He mean—the Kingdom of God? Jesus's whole message—His gospel—was about the KINGDOM OF GOD! Yet few know anything about it, today.

A kingdom is (a) a NATION composed of people, and (b) the GOVERNMENT of the nation. And a more complete eye-opening explanation will follow in Chapter 13.

In some cases, the people of a nation are the descendants—the children—of one man. The nation of Turkey was descended from ancient Esau, the twin brother of Jacob, whose name was changed to Israel. He was the father of the nation Israel. Before the twins were born, God said to their mother, Rebekah, "Two *nations* are in thy womb..." (Genesis 25:23).

Now Jesus the Messiah was to come as "the messenger of the COVENANT." The "Old Covenant" had established the human children of Israel as a NATION, or KINGDOM, of *humans*, called the KINGDOM OF ISRAEL. Jesus came as the Messenger—heralding the message of the NEW Covenant that shall set up the spirit-composed children of GOD as the Kingdom of God!

As the ancient kingdom of Israel was composed of the human FAMILY of the human man Israel, so the Kingdom of God will be composed of the *divine* Family of the divine God!

And what does this have to do with life after death? It has *everything* to do with it!

WHY JEWISH RULERS
REJECTED THE MESSAGE

The Jewish rulers of Jesus's day thought He was proclaiming a government to be set up immediately—to overthrow the Roman Empire, then ruling Judea as a vassal state.

One of these prominent Jews was a man named Nicodemus, mentioned earlier. He was a Pharisee, and the Pharisees were hostile to Jesus because of this new gospel. Nicodemus, however, wanted to meet this astonishing messenger and discuss it with Him. To avoid criticism from his colleagues, he came to Jesus by night.

"We know," he said, "that you are a teacher come from God."

The "we" implies that the divine identity of the Messenger and the source of His message was known to the Pharisees. But they were "NOW" people, concerned with protecting their status as rulers under the Roman government, not with receiving revelations from God.

Jesus perceived the import of Nicodemus's first words. His message was the good news of the coming WORLD GOVERNMENT of GOD—that is, the KINGDOM OF GOD, which shall rule all nations with the GOVERNMENT of God.

These Jewish rulers feared that message. Jesus was of their race—a Jew. If they did not oppose Him, they feared being shorn of their power and perhaps put to death as subversives threatening the overthrow of the Roman government. And the Pharisees thought Jesus proclaimed the *immediate* takeover of that rule!

NOT OF THIS AGE

Therefore Jesus did not waste words. He struck straight through to the crux point—the Kingdom of God is *not* of *this* world—this time, this age—but of the WORLD TOMORROW—a different and a following AGE. Not composed of humans, but of immortals—the GOD FAMILY!

So Jesus said, "Except a man be born again, he cannot see the kingdom of God" (John 3:3).

Notice carefully that being "born again" has a vital connection with the Kingdom of God—with THE FACT that it is not of this time—this age.

But Jesus's abrupt opening statement left Nicodemus confused. The religious leaders and the hundreds of denominations and sects professing Christianity today are confused and deceived! Today's religionists put a different twist on it than did Nicodemus, however.

Nicodemus *did* understand clearly what is meant by being *born*. He knew it meant being delivered from his mother's womb. It meant being delivered into the WORLD! Today's religious leaders read into it a different meaning! What Nicodemus could not understand was *how*—in what manner—anyone could be born AGAIN! And of course, being carnal-minded, he could only conceive of a second *physical* birth. But he *knew* what being *born* meant!

BORN HUMAN A SECOND TIME?

Puzzled, he asked, "How can a man be born when he is old? can he enter the second time into his mother's womb, and be born?" (verse 4). He was not confused about what is meant by being BORN. What Nicodemus could not understand was a *second* birth. He thought Jesus was talking about a second *human* birth.

He was unable to conceive of any but a second *physical* birth. His mind could not *grasp* spiritual things.

Now Jesus had made clear that the Kingdom of God is something that can be seen—but not until or UNLESS one is "born again." Not during his physical *lifetime!* Also, verse 5, the Kingdom of God is something a man may *enter into*—but not until after he is born AGAIN—another and entirely different birth.

Here is the crux point that explains it all: Jesus said, "That which is born of the flesh IS flesh; and that which is born of the Spirit IS *spirit*" (verse 6).

Man is now flesh—human. He is MATERIAL SUBSTANCE. "[D]ust thou art," said God to Adam, "and unto dust shalt thou return." Again, "And the [ETERNAL] God formed man of the dust of the ground, and breathed into his nostrils the breath of life; and man became a living soul" (Genesis 3:19; 2:7).

THOSE BORN AGAIN TO BE SPIRIT

But, said Jesus plainly, when one is born of the Spirit HE WILL *BE* SPIRIT! Look at it! Read it in your own Bible.

The Kingdom of God will be composed of SPIRIT BEINGS—not of humans!

At birth of human flesh, one is delivered from his mother's womb into *this* world. When born of the Spirit, one will be delivered from the CHURCH of God (physical)—the mother of begotten Christians—into the KINGDOM of God (a kingdom of SPIRIT BEINGS).

Man is now COMPOSED of flesh—material substance—matter. When BORN AGAIN he will *BE* spirit—a SPIRIT BEING, no longer human. He will be COMPOSED of spirit—of spirit composition—with life inherent—with self-containing life—not then existing by the breath of air and the circulation of blood.

Of the next age when the Kingdom of God will rule the world—the life after death—the next LIFE—Jesus said, "[T]hey neither marry, nor are given in marriage, but are *as* the angels of God ..." (Matthew 22:30). Marriage is a physical, fleshly union. In the age of God's Kingdom, when "born again" we shall BE spirit, not flesh. Born of God as SPIRIT BEINGS, no longer human. Angels are spirits—composed of spirit (Hebrews 1:7). Jesus did not say we shall then *be* angels—but AS the angels—sexless and composed of SPIRIT. Angels are spirit beings—created as such—but not begotten and BORN of God as God's own born children. We therefore shall be greater than angels!

Jesus explained this further to Nicodemus: "The wind bloweth were it listeth, and thou hearest the sound thereof, but canst not tell whence it cometh, and whither it goeth: so is everyone that is born of the Spirit" (John 3:8).

You cannot see wind. Wind is compared to spirit. It is INVISIBLE. That's why mortal FLESH, as we now are, cannot SEE the Kingdom of God. Those who inherit it will *be* spirit—normally invisible to eyes still human.

NOT WHILE FLESH AND BLOOD

The Apostle Paul made clear that the Kingdom of God is something a human may INHERIT, but not in THIS AGE—not while he is composed of material flesh.

"The first man is of the earth, earthy [human]: the second man is the Lord from heaven [a divine God Being]" (1 Corinthians 15:47).

This is what Jesus was saying to Nicodemus. He was of the earth, earthy—human. He was flesh, not spirit. He was born of the flesh, so that's what he was—FLESH. When one is born of the Spirit, he will BE spirit. Paul is here explaining the same truth.

But we cannot BE spirit in this present age.

THERE IS A TIME ELEMENT CONCERNED WITH BEING BORN AGAIN INTO GOD'S KINGDOM.

Continue, now, in 1 Corinthians 15: "And as we have borne the image of the earthy, we shall [future—resurrection] also bear the image of the heavenly" (verse 49). As we are now flesh, we shall be SPIRIT—at the resurrection, that is, when we shall be "BORN AGAIN"—when we shall *see,* enter into, the Kingdom of God—when we *are* spirit—at the resurrection!

"Now this I say, brethren, that flesh and blood cannot inherit the kingdom of God; neither doth corruption inherit incorruption. Behold, I shew you a mystery; We shall not all sleep [be dead], but we shall all be *changed,* In a moment, in the twinkling of an eye, at the last trump: for the trumpet shall sound, and the dead shall be raised incorruptible, and we [the then living] shall be *changed*" (verses 50-52). *There* is the TIME *when* we may be born again—*when* we may *see,* enter into, and inherit the Kingdom—when "BORN AGAIN," and *NOT BEFORE!*

How shall we be changed? The next words answer! "For this corruptible [flesh, as we now are] must put on incorruption [spirit—that which is born of God *is* spirit], and this mortal must put on immortality"—be changed from material flesh to spirit!

Until born again, we cannot *see* the Kingdom of God—Jesus to Nicodemus, John 3:3.

Until born again, we cannot *enter into* the Kingdom of God—Jesus to Nicodemus, John 3:5.

Until no longer flesh, but *changed* into SPIRIT, we cannot enter into the Kingdom of God—Jesus to Nicodemus, John 3:6-8.

While still flesh and blood (as Nicodemus was and we are) we cannot *inherit* the Kingdom of God—Paul to the Corinthians, 1 Corinthians 15:50.

Until the resurrection, at Christ's coming, we shall not be changed from corruptible flesh into incorruptible SPIRIT—Paul, 1 Corinthians 15:50-53 and verses 22-23.

Until the resurrection, therefore, we cannot *see, enter* into, or *inherit* the Kingdom of God. We CANNOT BE BORN AGAIN UNTIL THE RESURRECTION!

NOW HEIRS—NOT YET INHERITORS

While in our present status, born of the flesh and composed of flesh, we cannot see, enter into, or inherit the Kingdom of God. Notice, now, the status of the truly converted Christian, in this life—this world:

"… Now if any man have not the Spirit of Christ, he is none of his" (Romans 8:9). Unless one has received the Holy Spirit, and this Spirit is dwelling in him, he is not a Christian. Joining a church does not make one a Christian. Receiving and following God's Spirit does!

SPIRITUAL BIRTH PROCESS COMPARES TO PHYSICAL

But now see how God's Spirit entering and dwelling in one compares to the physical sperm impregnating the ovum— the imparting of eternal SPIRIT life, later to produce a SPIRIT PERSON! A fertilized ovum—an embryo—is NOT a *born* human person. Life from the father has been imparted to it. He has begotten it, but neither embryo nor fetus is YET a *born* person. In the same manner the Spirit-begotten human is not, *yet*, a SPIRIT PERSON or BEING, as Jesus said he shall be *when* born again!

Continue: "But if the Spirit of him that raised up Jesus from the dead dwell in you, he that raised up Christ from the dead shall also quicken your mortal bodies by his Spirit that dwelleth in you" (verse 11).

UNDERSTAND THIS! There is a direct comparison between having been born of the flesh and being born AGAIN of God. Jesus said that which is born of the flesh *is* flesh—a born *human*. That which is born of the Spirit (God) *is* spirit—a born SPIRIT PERSON!

A mortal human life *starts* when a sperm cell from the body of the father impregnates—imparts physical LIFE to—an ovum (egg cell) in the mother. At this point the father begets, sires. He does not "bring forth." The mother does that, later. His part in the PROCESS leading to final birth is then *done*. BUT THERE IS A TIME ELEMENT. At the TIME of begettal, birth (parturition) has not YET occurred.

It is necessary to give this explanation, at this point, because the popular deception of a deceived traditional "Christianity" is to claim that when one "receives Christ," "accepts Christ," "professes Christ," or first receives God's Holy Spirit to dwell in him, he is already "BORN AGAIN."

First, then, notice the physical type and comparison.

THE TIME ELEMENT

In human physical reproduction, there is a TIME ELEMENT. From impregnation—*begettal* on the part of the father—having *conceived* on the part of the mother—to BIRTH, or *parturition*, or being delivered from the mother's womb is a TIME ELEMENT of nine months.

That nine-month period is called *gestation*. Upon conception, the now fertilized *ovum* is called an *embryo*. A few months later, it is called a fetus. But *during* this nine-month period of *gestation*, we do not speak of the embryo-fetus as having been *born*. It is in the PROCESS toward birth. It is the child of its parents. But it is then the *unborn* child of its parents. The father has already begotten it—sired it. But the mother has not yet given *birth* to it. Yet it is, during the gestation period, the *unborn* child of its parents.

Now in being "born again," the PROCESS of this birth begins when GOD's divine SPIRIT-LIFE is imparted to us by the Holy Spirit, from His very PERSON, entering to dwell within us. Repeat, from Romans 8: "But if the Spirit of him that raised up Jesus from the dead dwell in you, he that raised up

Christ from the dead shall also quicken [change to immortal spirit] your mortal bodies by his Spirit that dwelleth in you" (verse 11). This is describing the very same thing explained in 1 Corinthians 15:50-53, the resurrection.

I want to make this crystal clear. Millions of sincere professing Christians believe that when they profess Christ (or receive His Holy Spirit) they are "born again." What actually happens is this:

When one, after repentance, faith, and baptism receives the Holy Spirit, the Spirit of God puts him into—baptizes him into—God's Church. The Church is called the Body of Christ. So we read: "[B]y one Spirit are we all baptized into one body…" (1 Corinthians 12:13).

THE CHURCH OUR MOTHER

Again, the Church is called "Jerusalem above" or "the heavenly Jerusalem" (Hebrews 12:22-23). Now notice, in Galatians 4:26: "But Jerusalem which is above is free, which is the mother of us all."

The analogy is this: When begotten by God the Father by receiving His Holy Spirit, we are put into the Church, which during this gestation period is our MOTHER.

The human mother of the fetus within her womb serves the function of feeding her unborn child with physical food, so that it may develop and grow physically. And also she carries it where she may best protect it from physical injury or harm, until parturition—delivery from her womb.

The spiritual mother—the Church—is commissioned to "feed the flock" (1 Peter 5:2) through the ministry which God has set in the Church "[f]or the perfecting of the saints… for the edifying of the body of Christ: Till we all come in the unity of the faith, and of the knowledge of the Son of God, unto a perfect man…" (Ephesians 4:11-13). Just as the human fetus develops and grows physically during the PRE-birth gestation period, so WE, after begettal by God's Spirit, develop and grow SPIRITUALLY in PRE-birth state.

Human life *starts* with what the Bible terms "corruptible seed"—physical male sperm. Divine life *starts* with that which is incorruptible—the Holy Spirit of God entering the human person. But as the human embryo must GROW till it becomes a fetus, which must GROW to the point of being born into the human family, *so* the Christian in whom divine life has been started by the gift of God's *incorruptible* Spirit must GROW toward perfection to be born into the GOD Family. He will *then* be perfect, unable to sin.

But—that perfection of holy righteous CHARACTER must be developed (with God's help and the in-filling of His Spirit during this *human* life—the spiritual "gestation" stage).

But not only is the Church to feed the members on the Word of God—spiritual food—but also to protect these conceived but yet unborn children of God from spiritual harm, as the very next verse shows: "That we henceforth be no more children, tossed to and fro, and carried about with every wind of doctrine, by the sleight of men, and cunning craftiness, whereby they lie in wait to deceive" (verse 14).

Then, at the time of the resurrection, we in the Church—the spiritual mother—shall be DELIVERED from her, and born into—brought forth into—the Kingdom, the spirit-composed FAMILY of God.

SONS OF GOD NOW

Now, further: "For as many as are led by the Spirit of God, they are the sons of God" (Romans 8:14). The unborn child in his mother's womb is the child of his father and mother, though not *yet* born—delivered from the womb. So are we, if God's Spirit dwells in us—if we are being led by God's Spirit—children of God. Yet, at *this time*, we are in the *gestation* state, not yet *parturition*. And only HEIRS, not inheritors!

Continue: "And if children, then heirs; heirs of God, and joint-heirs with Christ; if so be that we suffer with him, that we may be [future—at resurrection] also glorified together" (verse 17).

Now see how this passage designates the resurrection into GLORY, when we shall BE spirit, as a BIRTH!

"For the earnest expectation of the [creation] waiteth for the manifestation of the sons of God"—that is *the time* of Christ's coming to REIGN and of the resurrection to SPIRIT composition—"...Because the [creation] itself also *shall be delivered [a birth]* from the bondage of corruption into the glorious liberty of the children of God. For we know that the whole creation groaneth and *travaileth in pain* together until now" (verses 19-22).

Here is another comparison. We shall be delivered from *this world* (the Church is *in*, though not *of*, this world) into the glorious WORLD TOMORROW and the Kingdom which shall rule it.

The CREATION is waiting for this time of Christ's coming, the resurrection, and the Kingdom of God, because the creation *shall be DELIVERED* from the bondage of corruption, or deteriorated decay. It is not now delivered. It SHALL BE—at the resurrection. Although this is not referring directly to *our* being born again, it IS a direct comparison to the BIRTH of a child being DELIVERED from its mother's womb.

The resurrection—the time when we are changed to BE spirit and to INHERIT the Kingdom—will be a time of DELIVERY FROM the bondage of corruptible flesh and from this world of SIN—A REAL BIRTH!

CHRIST BORN A SECOND TIME BY THE RESURRECTION

Continue in Romans 8: "For whom he did foreknow, he also did predestinate to be conformed to the image of his Son, that he [Jesus] might be the first*born* among many brethren" (verse 29).

Now compare with Romans 1:3-4: "Concerning his Son Jesus Christ our Lord, which was made of the seed of David according to the flesh; And declared to be the Son of God ... by the resurrection from the dead."

Jesus was, in the human flesh—His first birth—a descendant of David. But, by the resurrection from the dead (born AGAIN), Jesus became the born Son of God, now no longer human, but composed of SPIRIT—a Spirit Being. He thus became the FIRST SO BORN of many brethren who *shall be* BORN AGAIN at the time of the resurrection of those who are Christ's.

Of course we understand, and so did Paul in writing the above, that Jesus was also the Son of God while in the human flesh. Though *born of a human* woman, He was sired by God. But this is comparing the two births: the one from the human Mary, as descended from the human David, and the other, by His resurrection to glory, as Son of God.

Emphatically this does NOT imply that Jesus was a sinner needing salvation. He was the Pioneer, setting us the example, that we, too, may be BORN of God.

WHEN BORN AGAIN,
WHAT SHALL WE BE LIKE?

When we are born again, what shall we be like? The Bible gives us the answer: "For our conversation [citizenship] is in heaven; *from whence* also we look for the Saviour, the Lord Jesus Christ: Who shall *change* our vile body [FLESH], that it may be fashioned like unto his glorious body ..." (Philippians 3:20-21).

Now notice a scripture in the third chapter of 1 John. Here it plainly says that "WE"—meaning begotten, converted Christians—are now, already, the SONS of God, as was explained earlier. Next, this scripture reveals that "it doth not yet appear WHAT WE SHALL BE" (1 John 3:2). We are, later, to be something different. As Jesus explained to Nicodemus, we SHALL BE immortal spirit. That is what we shall later be.

"[B]ut," this scripture continues—read it—understand this WONDERFUL TRUTH—"we know that, when he [Christ] shall appear [at His Second Coming to Earth], WE SHALL BE LIKE HIM ...." We shall look like Christ!

What does the GLORIFIED Christ look like? His eyes blaze forth like flames of fire! His feet glow like finely burnished brass. His face shines like the SUN, in FULL STRENGTH—so bright it would blind your eyes if He were visible to you now! (Revelation 1:14-16; 19:12-13; Matthew 17:2).

And THAT is the way YOU and I shall look if and when we are finally BORN of GOD!

OUR TRANSCENDENT POTENTIAL

There is another passage, understood by almost none, that reveals our astonishing *transcendent* potential! It begins in Hebrews 2:6: "What is man, that thou art mindful of him? ..."

Even though this was covered in greater detail in Chapter 3, it is important that it be summarized in connection with the subject of this chapter—life after death.

Yes, why should the great God be concerned about us mortals? WHY did He put us here on Earth? What is the PURPOSE of life? What is our transcendent potential? It is so far above and beyond anything you have thought or imagined, it seems shockingly incredible!

Can you believe it? Are you willing to believe what is now plainly stated? Here comes the astonishing answer, beginning verse 7:

"Thou madest him a little lower than the angels...." Some translations have it, "for a little while lower than the angels." Continue: "[T]hou crownedst him [kingship] with GLORY and honour, and didst set him over the works of thy hands"—that is, God's creation.

NOT YET THE UNIVERSE!

"Thou hast put ALL THINGS [Moffatt: the universe] in subjection under his feet. For in that he put ALL in subjection under him, he *left nothing* that is not put under him" (verse 8). Can you grasp that? The entire, vast, endless UNIVERSE! But that is for BORN sons of God. Man is not yet BORN—except Christ only! Continue: Here comes the answer:

"...But *now* [in this present gestation state] we see NOT YET all things [the universe] put under him."

But what *do* we see, NOW?

"But we see JESUS... crowned with glory and honour..." (verse 9). Yes, Jesus has already been given the executive administration of God's government—the KINGDOM OF GOD—over the entire UNIVERSE! Only, *until* our time to inherit and possess the government of EARTH, at Christ's return, He is allowing Satan to continue on this Earth his work of deception. Now continue:

"For it became him [Jesus], for whom are all things, and by whom are all things, in bringing many sons unto GLORY, to make the captain [margin—leader, forerunner, or pioneer—the one who has gone on before us, as we are to follow] of their salvation perfect through sufferings. For both he that sanctifieth and they who are sanctified are all of one: for which cause he is not ashamed to call them *brethren*" (verses 10-11).

CHRIST OUR ELDER BROTHER

We are, as quoted before, heirs of God, and joint-heirs—as BRETHREN—with Christ. He has gone on ahead, through a resurrection, to GLORY as the Pioneer!

He is the firstborn of many brethren! He has INHERITED "all things"—the UNIVERSE! We are still heirs—still in the gestation stage of the process of being BORN of God. Jesus is now our Elder Brother and High Priest, supervising our spiritual development—preparing us to be kings and priests, reigning *with* Him!

The first thousand years we shall reign ON THE EARTH. For He shall have "made them [kings] and priests to our God, and they shall reign on earth" (Revelation 5:10, RSV).

RULING WITH CHRIST

For that first thousand years, Jesus is to reign on the throne of His earthly ancestor DAVID in Jerusalem (Isaiah 9:6-7). And "he that overcometh, and keepeth my works unto the end, to him will I give power over the nations: And he shall rule them with a rod of iron…" (Revelation 2:26-27). But how and from where shall we rule?

Jesus said, again, "To him that overcometh will I grant to sit with me in my throne [at Jerusalem], even as I also overcame, and am [now] set down with my Father in his throne" (Revelation 3:21).

When BORN of God, we shall BE spirit, no longer human flesh and blood. We shall be given POWER!

As Daniel revealed, the saints then shall take the kingdoms of Earth's nations and rule them for the first thousand years— establishing WORLD PEACE and divine government under Christ.

And after that? The passage in Hebrews 2 shows that then, again under Christ, we shall be given power to rule over the entire vast universe—literally all things. For that is the power that has been given to Christ and will be ours as joint inheritors with Him!

Yes, there is a LIFE AFTER DEATH for those obedient to God—a spirit life of incredible potential beyond our wildest dreams! Can we humans grasp the awesome portent of these astounding truths? Attaining immortal life should be our all-encompassing goal. For that is the gift and desire of our merciful Father and His Son Jesus Christ.

Chapter 13
World Peace— How It Will Come

ITRAVEL TO ALL PARTS OF THE WORLD AS AN AMBASSADOR (WITHOUT political portfolio) for WORLD PEACE. I discuss world problems, evils and world peace with many heads of governments—kings, presidents, prime ministers, and those high in the government, leaders in science, education, commerce and industry. I have not been called, and therefore make no effort, to bring about world peace—but serve as an ambassador of the power *that will* bring it in our time!

Most world leaders are of superior ability. Yet they are utterly unable to abolish world evils or bring about world *peace*.

Many scientists and leaders say that the only hope for world peace is the formation of a supreme WORLD GOVERNMENT, controlling the world's sole military power. Yet in the same breath they admit the utter impossibility of this, claiming that such supreme world power in human hands would enslave us all!

AN AMAZING FORECAST

Few realize it today, but centuries ago a famous personage issued a pronouncement forecasting this very solution. He was hundreds of years ahead of his time, and the world of his day rejected and suppressed the pronouncement. The world soon lost knowledge of his forecast.

World leaders would do well to search out that amazing forecast, in the light of present world conditions.

I have been privileged to announce to many of the world's "great and near-great" this world's only hope—SURE HOPE—to occur in *our time!*

Few, indeed, know that Jesus Christ came, not as a religious leader on a "soul saving" crusade, but as a pioneer NEWS FORECASTER. No man of historic note has been so completely misrepresented—so utterly misunderstood!

He came as a MESSENGER with a MESSAGE from God Almighty to mankind. His message was BIG NEWS—a vital and sensational news ANNOUNCEMENT for the future. It announced world peace. It was good news for the future, proclaimed as an advance ANNOUNCEMENT OF ASSURED AND CERTAIN WORLD PEACE in OUR TIME. That was Christ's GOSPEL! The very word "gospel" *means* "good news."

And what was that news announcement for our times which was suppressed by first-century enemies? The one official record which the first-century conspirators were unable to suppress—the Holy BIBLE—gives the official answer!

"The beginning of the gospel of Jesus Christ, the Son of God .... Jesus came into Galilee, preaching the *gospel* of the kingdom of God, And saying, The time is fulfilled, and the KINGDOM OF GOD is at hand: repent ye, and believe the gospel" (Mark 1:1, 14-15).

Believe *what* gospel—*wha*t GOOD NEWS? The good news of the coming KINGDOM OF GOD.

But what did He *mean*—the KINGDOM OF GOD? And how do we know it was suppressed? And if the original and *true* gospel of Jesus Christ was suppressed, what gospel or gospels were proclaimed to the world to replace it?

THE WRITTEN RECORD

To say that the true gospel proclaimed by Christ was suppressed—was not proclaimed to the world after A.D. 70 for nearly 19 centuries—is, indeed, a shocking and amazing statement.

This same written record the conspirators were not able to destroy confirms it. The Church of God was started the day of Pentecost, A.D. 31 (Acts 2). About 20 years later, the Apostle Paul, under inspiration, wrote to the churches in Galatia,

"I marvel that ye are so soon removed from him that called you into the grace of Christ *unto another gospel:* Which is not another; but there be some that trouble you, and would *pervert the gospel of Christ*" (Galatians 1:6-7). The verses following pronounce a double curse on any who would preach any other gospel.

To the Corinthian church the Apostle Paul wrote, "...I fear, lest by any means, as the serpent beguiled Eve through his subtilty, so your minds should be corrupted from the simplicity that is in Christ. For if he that cometh [speaking of false preachers] preacheth *another Jesus...* or *another gospel,* which ye have not accepted...*" (2 Corinthians 11:3-4).

And further—verses 13-15: "For such are false apostles, deceitful workers, transforming themselves into the apostles of Christ. And no marvel; for Satan himself is transformed into an angel of light. Therefore it is no great thing if his *ministers* also be transformed as the ministers of righteousness...."

To the early Christians at Rome: "For the wrath of God is revealed from heaven against all ungodliness and unrighteousness of men, who *hold* [*back*] the truth in unrighteousness" (Romans 1:18). The Revised Standard Version has it: "who by their wickedness *suppress the truth.*" The message God sent by Jesus Christ was being *held back—suppressed.*

Then again, even Jesus Christ Himself made it very clear that His gospel—the KINGDOM OF GOD—would be suppressed *until* our time.

His disciples had asked what would be the sign by which we might know when we were at the end of this world (age), just before Christ's return to Earth.

First He warned them against being deceived. Many would come, He said, in His name, claiming to be the ministers of Christ saying that He—Jesus—was the Christ and at the same time deceiving the many. But when "...this *gospel of the kingdom* shall be preached in all the world for a witness unto all nations... *then* shall the end come" (Matthew 24:14).

This proclaiming of the KINGDOM OF GOD could not be the sign that we are at the end of the age, if it *had been* proclaimed all along!

Just as Christ Himself directly prophesied would happen, many have preached about the *person,* saying that Jesus was the Christ—preaching about the Messenger, but SUPPRESSING His message!

But the END TIME is now here. After almost 19 centuries, that message is now going out WORLDWIDE, by the one true Church of God!

Some have preached a "gospel of salvation" (actually a false salvation) and some a "gospel of grace"—turning grace into license to commit sin. Still others have turned to a "social gospel."

But Jesus brought from God the Father a vital message announcing the KINGDOM OF GOD! What did He mean—the KINGDOM OF GOD? Isn't it amazing that almost no one in today's world knows?

A MESSAGE OF GOVERNMENT

Few seem to know, today, that Jesus's MESSAGE was about GOVERNMENT! Few realize that this is NOT the time God is trying to SAVE (spiritually) the world. Few knew Jesus was concerned with GOVERNMENT.

Jesus was born to be a KING! Notice, once again, what was prophesied in Isaiah about Christ: "For unto us a child is born, unto us a son is given: and the GOVERNMENT shall be upon his shoulder: and his name shall be called Wonderful, Counsellor, The mighty God, The everlasting Father, The Prince of Peace. Of the increase of his GOVERNMENT and peace there shall be no end, upon the throne of David, and upon his kingdom, to order it, and to establish it with judgment and with justice from henceforth even for ever" (Isaiah 9:6-7).

Notice what was said to his mother Mary: "... the angel Gabriel was sent from God unto ... Nazareth, To a virgin espoused to a man whose name was Joseph, of the house of David; and the virgin's name was Mary. And the angel came in unto her, and said, Hail, thou that art highly favoured .... [T]hou shalt conceive in thy womb, and bring forth a son, and shalt call his name Jesus. He shall be great, and shall be called the Son of the Highest: and the Lord God shall give unto him *the throne* of his father David: And he *shall reign* over the house of Jacob for ever; and of his KINGDOM there shall be no end" (Luke 1:26-33).

When Jesus was on trial for His life before Pilate, He was asked, "Art thou a king then?" Jesus answered, "Thou sayest I am a king. To this end was I born, and for this cause came I into the world…." But He also said, "My kingdom is not of *this world*…" (John 18:37, 36).

WHY has the whole world been deceived, not knowing WHY humanity was created and human life existed upon this Earth?

Again, and again, I ask, *WHY* are we *HERE? WHERE* are we *GOING? WHAT* is the *WAY*—the WAY TO PEACE, well-being, happiness, abundance?

WHY no world PEACE? *Why* all this world's evils? *WHY* can't SCIENCE give us the answers? These questions are the MOST IMPORTANT in human life. WHY aren't people concerned?

The greatest religion in the world, in number of adherents, is Christianity. People SUPPOSE the Christian religion came out of—is based on—the BIBLE.

Then *WHY* don't the various sects and denominations of traditional Christianity tell us the REAL THEME of the Bible? WHY do they not know the TRUE GOSPEL that Jesus proclaimed? It's all *IN THE BIBLE*—it's not suppressed *THERE!* It's plain and clear!

It's time someone SHOUTED to lethargic, indifferent, sleeping humanity, *WAKE UP!*

IS THERE AN AFTERLIFE?

Some fundamentalist denominations of Christianity preach about spiritual salvation—about an afterlife.

IS there an afterlife? The truth is PLAIN AND CLEAR in the Bible. And this was clarified in Chapter 12.

Jesus's gospel was the KINGDOM OF GOD. Does that have anything to do with *after*life—with spiritual salvation? It has *everything* to do with it. BUT THE WHOLE WORLD IS *DECEIVED* and *ASLEEP!* The gospel of the KINGDOM OF GOD has to do, basically, with TWO themes—government and spiritual salvation (which some call being "born again"). The previous chapter dealt with being "born again." This chapter deals with GOVERNMENT.

But once again, what did Jesus *mean,* THE KINGDOM OF GOD? The truth is not merely surprising—it is shocking—staggering! Yet it is truly GOOD NEWS—the most glorious GOOD NEWS ever to enter human consciousness!

CHRIST'S GOSPEL

Jesus went everywhere preaching the GOOD NEWS of the KINGDOM OF GOD. He taught in parables about the KINGDOM OF GOD. He sent out 70 men preaching, and commanded them to preach THE KINGDOM OF GOD (Luke 10:9). He sent the apostles, on whom the Church of God was founded, to preach only THE KINGDOM OF GOD (Luke 9:1-2).

Isn't it amazing that the world has LOST the knowledge of what it is?

The Apostle Paul preached THE KINGDOM OF GOD (Acts 19:8; 20:25; 28:23, 31).

Haven't you heard men speak of the Kingdom of God something like this: "By Christians everywhere working together to bring about world peace, tolerance and brotherly love, the Kingdom of God may at last be established in the hearts of men."

Because they *rejected* Christ's gospel 1,900 years ago, the world had to supplant something else in its place. They had to invent a *counterfeit!* So we have heard the Kingdom of God spoken of as merely a pretty platitude—a nice sentiment in human hearts—reducing it to an ethereal, unreal NOTHING! Others have misrepresented that the "CHURCH" is the Kingdom. Others confuse it with a "millennium." Still others have, earlier in our century, claimed the British Empire is the Kingdom of God. HOW DECEIVED CAN THIS WORLD GET?

DANIEL KNEW!

The Prophet Daniel, who lived 600 years before Christ, knew that the Kingdom of God was a real kingdom—a *government* ruling over literal PEOPLE on the Earth.

Daniel was one of four extraordinary, intelligent and brilliant Jewish lads in the Judean captivity. These four men were stationed in the palace of King Nebuchadnezzar of the Chaldean Empire, in training for special responsibilities in the Babylonian government. Daniel was a prophet who had been given special understanding in visions and dreams (Daniel 1:17).

Nebuchadnezzar was the first real world ruler. He had conquered a vast empire, including the nation Judah. This king had a dream so impressive it troubled him—moved him to tremendous concern. He demanded that his magicians, astrologers and sorcerers tell him both *what* he had dreamed, and what it meant. They could not. They were baffled. Then Daniel was brought before the king.

Daniel disclaimed any more human ability to interpret dreams than the Chaldean magicians, "BUT," he said, "there is a GOD in heaven that revealeth secrets, and maketh known to the king Nebuchadnezzar what shall be in the latter days" (Daniel 2:28).

First, God's purpose was to reveal to this world-ruling human king that there is a GOD in heaven—that GOD IS SUPREME RULER over all nations, governments and kings—that God RULES THE UNIVERSE! This Chaldean king knew only about the many pagan demon gods. He knew nothing of the true *living* ALMIGHTY God. Like people and rulers, even today, he did not know that GOD is the living, REAL, active, RULING and GOVERNING PERSONAGE who actually and literally *governs* the ENTIRE UNIVERSE!

The whole purpose of this DREAM was to *reveal* GOD's GOVERNMENT—the *fact* that God RULES—the truth of THE KINGDOM OF GOD—the very thing that is the one and *only* true GOSPEL OF JESUS CHRIST! And, secondly, to reveal—preserved in writing for us TODAY—what is to happen *"in the latter days"!*

FOR US, TODAY!

This is no dry, dull, dead writing for a people of 2,500 years ago. This is LIVING, TREMENDOUS, *BIG NEWS* for *OUR DAY!* It is *advance news* for us, *NOW.* News *before it happens*—of the most colossal event of all Earth's history certain to occur *in your life-time*—during the very next few years!

This is THE TRUE GOSPEL! It is the very gospel Christ preached! It is intended for you and me TODAY! It is vital that you UNDERSTAND!

Read, in your own Bible, verses 28 through 35. In his dream, this king had seen a vast statue—larger than any image or statue ever built by man—so tremendous it was terrifying, even in a dream. Its head was of fine gold, its breast and arms of silver, the belly and thighs of brass, legs of solid iron, feet a mixture of iron and clay.

There was a time element. Nebuchadnezzar had viewed it *until* a supernatural STONE came from heaven, smashing the statue on its feet. Then the whole of the statue broke into fragments, and was actually blown away by the wind—it disappeared! Then this STONE expanded miraculously and quickly became a great MOUNTAIN—so great it filled the whole Earth!

What did it mean? *Did* it have meaning? Yes, because this was God's doing. Unlike ordinary dreams, this one was caused by God to convey the message of God's sovereignty to Nebuchadnezzar—and, because it is part of the written Word of God, to us today—to reveal important facts of the TRUE GOSPEL!

"This is the dream," said Daniel (verse 36), "and we will tell the interpretation thereof before the king."

This, then, is GOD'S interpretation. It is decidedly *not* Herbert W. Armstrong's interpretation. Men ought never to *interpret* the Bible. The Bible gives us GOD'S OWN INTERPRETATION! Here it is:

"Thou, O king, art a king of kings"—he was the first real WORLD RULER over a world empire!—"…for the God of heaven hath given thee a kingdom, power, and strength, and glory" (verse 37). God was revealing Himself to this human world-dictator as the MOST HIGH *Ruler over all.*

People today, like this Chaldean king, seem never to think of God as a RULER—as the Supreme One who GOVERNS—as the Head of GOVERNMENT. The Eternal was revealing Himself through Daniel to Nebuchadnezzar—and through the Bible *to you and to me* TODAY—as a SOVEREIGN, ALL-POWERFUL, *GOVERNING* GOD who *is to be obeyed!*

"Thou," continued Daniel to this human emperor, "art this head of gold. And after thee shall arise another KINGDOM inferior to thee, and another third KINGDOM of brass, which shall bear rule over all the earth" (verses 38-39).

WHAT IS A KINGDOM?

Notice! This is speaking of KINGDOMS. It is referring to kingdoms *that bear rule over the people on Earth.* It is speaking of

GOVERNMENTS! It is not speaking of ethereal sentiments "set up in the hearts of men." It is not speaking of churches. It is speaking of the kind of GOVERNMENTS that bear RULE and AUTHORITY over nations of PEOPLE here on Earth. It is literal. It is specific. There is no misunderstanding, here, as to what is meant by the word "KINGDOM."

There is no misunderstanding the interpretation. GOD gives His own interpretation through the Prophet Daniel. The great metallic image represented national and international GOVERN-MENTS—real, literal KINGDOMS.

It represented a *succession* of world-ruling governments. First was the head of gold. That represented Nebuchadnezzar and his kingdom—the Chaldean Empire. *After* him—later, in time sequence—was to come a second, then a third KINGDOM "which shall bear RULE over all the earth"—*world empire!*

Then, verse 40, the legs of iron represent a *fourth* world empire. It was to be *strong*, even as iron is strong—stronger militarily than its predecessors. Yet, as silver is less valuable than gold, brass than silver, iron than brass, though each metal was progressively harder and stronger, the succession would deteriorate morally and spiritually. The two legs meant the fourth empire would be divided.

After the Chaldean Empire came the still larger Persian Empire, then the Greco-Macedonian, and fourth, the Roman Empire. It was divided, with capitals at Rome and Constantinople.

Now—verse 44! Read it! Get your Bible. See it with your own eyes in your own Bible. Here, in PLAIN LANGUAGE, is God's explanation of what the KINGDOM OF GOD IS:

"And in the days of these kings…"—it is here speaking of the 10 toes, part of iron and part of brittle clay. This, by con-necting the prophecy with Daniel 7, and Revelation 13 and 17, is referring to the new UNITED STATES OF EUROPE which is *now forming,* before your very eyes! Revelation 17:12 makes plain the detail that it shall be a union of TEN KINGS OR KINGDOMS which (Revelation 17:8) shall resurrect the medieval "Holy" ROMAN EMPIRE.

So, mark carefully the *time element!* "[I]n the days of these kings"—in the days of these 10 nations or groups of nations that shall, *IN OUR TIME,* resurrect briefly the Roman

Empire—notice what shall happen: "...shall the God of heaven set up a kingdom, which shall never be destroyed...but it shall break in pieces and consume all these kingdoms, and it shall stand for ever"! (Daniel 2:44).

YES, IN OUR TIME!

Now here we have described FOUR universal empires—the *only* four that ever existed! Revelation 13 and 17 show that, after the fall of the original Roman Empire, there would be 10 revivals—SEVEN of which would be ruled over by a Gentile CHURCH—the "daughter" of ancient BABYLON—a church claiming to be Christian, but actually named by God "MYSTERY BABYLON the Great"—or, more plainly, BABYLONIAN MYSTERIES!

Six of those have come and gone. The seventh is now forming—the last, final, *brief* resurrection of the Roman Empire by 10 European groups or nations. These are the 10 toes of iron and clay mixed.

In their days—and they shall last but a *very* short space, possibly no more than two to three-and-a-half years—shall the GOD OF HEAVEN SET UP *A KINGDOM.*

This, then, shall be THE KINGDOM OF GOD!

Compare with Revelation 17. Here is pictured a church. Not a small church—a GREAT church. She rules over "many waters" (verse 1), which are described in verse 15 as different nations speaking different languages. She posed as the Church of GOD—which Scripture says (Ephesians 5:23; Revelation 19:7; Matthew 25:1-10, etc.) is the affianced "Bride" of CHRIST, to be spiritually MARRIED to Him at His Second COMING.

But she has committed fornication. How? By having direct *political* union with HUMAN GOVERNMENTS of THIS WORLD! She "sat on" (Revelation 17:3) all seven of these resurrections of the Roman Empire—called the "Holy Roman Empire." She RULED OVER the human kingdoms—as a common-law and unmarried "wife" ruling her paramour "husband"—a totally unnatural and ungodly relationship.

She is, therefore, to "sit on" this last "head of the beast"—this final resurrection of the "Holy Roman Empire." It will be a *union* of church and state. It is to endure but a *very* short time. It is to FIGHT AGAINST CHRIST at His SECOND COMING! That will be its END.

We see it in process of rising, now. Therefore we are CLOSE to the coming of Christ! We are now *very near* the END of this world!

When Christ comes, He is coming as KING of kings, ruling the whole Earth (Revelation 19:11-16), and His KINGDOM—*the KINGDOM OF GOD*—said Daniel, is to CONSUME all these worldly kingdoms.

Revelation 11:15 states it in these words: "The kingdoms of this world *are become* THE KINGDOMS OF OUR LORD, AND OF HIS CHRIST; and he shall reign for ever and ever"!

This is THE KINGDOM OF GOD. It is the END of present governments—the governments that rule Russia, China, Japan, Italy, Germany—yes, and even the United States and the British nations. They then shall *become* the kingdoms—the GOVERNMENTS—of the Lord JESUS CHRIST, then KING of kings over the entire Earth.

This makes completely PLAIN the fact that the KINGDOM OF GOD is a literal GOVERNMENT. Even as the Chaldean Empire was a KINGDOM—even as the Roman Empire was a KINGDOM—so the KINGDOM OF GOD is a government. It is to *take over* the GOVERNMENT of the NATIONS of the world.

Jesus Christ was BORN to be a KING—a RULER!

These Scriptures tell you PLAINLY *that* GOD is supreme RULER. They tell you in plainest language that Jesus was born to be a KING—that He is going to RULE ALL NATIONS OF THE EARTH—that His Kingdom shall rule eternally.

But all this is only *part* of the fantastic, amazing, actually SHOCKING TRUTH about the KINGDOM OF GOD.

The KINGDOM OF GOD will rule *over* the peoples and nations of the Earth. Yet these mortal peoples and nations will NOT be the Kingdom, not even *in* the Kingdom of God. They shall be merely RULED OVER BY IT!

We still have to learn OF WHAT or OF WHOM it is composed. Can *YOU*, as an individual, ever become *a part* of this Kingdom?

CAN BE ENTERED!

In Jesus's day, the religious leaders *knew* He was a teacher sent from God with GOD's TRUTH. They branded Him a false prophet, heretic, and seditionist. Yet *they knew* His was the voice of GOD!

One of them, a Pharisee named Nicodemus, occupying an office of authority over the Jews, came secretly by night to see Jesus. In Chapter 12, one phase of Nicodemus's night visit with Jesus was covered; but now, MORE!

"Rabbi," said this Pharisee, "we know that thou art a teacher come from God ..." (John 3:2). Yes, *we Pharisees*, he said, *know that!* He did not say "I know it." He said *"WE know"*—we *Pharisees!* They knew He spoke the TRUTH—yet they not only rejected it, they crucified Him!

But Jesus hewed straight to the line! He told Nicodemus about THE KINGDOM OF GOD. He told him some things you need to UNDERSTAND!

Notice! "Jesus answered and said unto him, Verily, verily, I say unto thee, Except a man be born again, he cannot see the kingdom of God" (verse 3). Yes, notice! The Kingdom of God is something that CAN be seen, but only by those who have been "born again." It is something others *cannot see!* Read it in Chapter 12, or request our free booklet *Just What Do You Mean ... Born Again?*

But what about the CHURCH? Can carnal people who make no claim to having been "born again" SEE A CHURCH? Of course! But they *cannot* see the Kingdom of God! So SAID JESUS! Then, if you believe Jesus, the CHURCH cannot be the Kingdom of God!

Notice further: "Jesus answered, Verily, verily, I say unto thee, Except a man be born of water and of the Spirit, he cannot enter into the kingdom of God" (verse 5). The Kingdom of God is something that *can be entered into*—BUT, only those "born of water and of the Spirit" can enter into it!

Notice further! In the resurrection chapter of the Bible, we read: "Now this I say, brethren, that flesh and blood cannot inherit the kingdom of God; neither doth corruption inherit incorruption" (1 Corinthians 15:50). The Kingdom of God is something no human, of flesh and blood, can enter or *inherit!*

Now do flesh-and-blood people enter into the CHURCH? If so, then the Kingdom of God *cannot* be the CHURCH—for the Kingdom of God is something flesh-and-blood humans *cannot enter into!*

What do you think the "Church" is? Is it the building? Flesh-and-blood people can and do enter buildings and cathedrals called "churches." Is it the converted PEOPLE? Flesh-and-blood people can and DO enter into the membership of any group of PEOPLE that may call itself the Church. But flesh and blood *cannot* enter the Kingdom of GOD—so the CHURCH *is not the Kingdom of God!*

IN MEN'S HEARTS?

Now some think the Kingdom of God is some ethereal sentimental feeling or something set up in men's hearts. If so, then the Kingdom of God enters into mortal man. But these plain scriptures say that it is men after they are no longer flesh and blood—but resurrected into spirit-composed bodies—who can *enter into* the Kingdom of God. It does not enter into men. Men enter into it—*after* they are resurrected in glory—*after* they are no longer "flesh and blood."

Is it the "god within you"? Absolutely not. It is not something that was born inside of man, or that has ever entered into man. It is something man may enter *after* he is "born again."

What about the British Empire? Well, I have been pretty well over the British Isles, Canada and Australia—and all of the multi-thousands I have seen there were flesh-and-blood humans. They *did* enter the British Empire—no longer extant—but they *cannot* enter the Kingdom of God, in their present flesh-and-blood life. So the British Empire *cannot* be the Kingdom of God.

But, someone misunderstanding the scripture may ask, "Didn't Jesus Himself say that the Kingdom of God is '*within you*'?" In the 17th chapter of Luke, verse 21, King James translation, is a MISTRANSLATION which has led some to suppose the Kingdom of God is some thought or feeling or sentiment within man.

IN HEARTS OF PHARISEES?

Let's take a good look at this. First realize, if it does say that, it is contradicted by all the other scriptures I am giving you. If the Bible does contradict itself, you can't believe it anyway—so then it still would prove nothing.

First, *to whom* is Jesus speaking? Read it!

"And when he was demanded of the Pharisees, when the kingdom of God should come, he answered them and said, The kingdom of God cometh not with observation: Neither shall they say, Lo here! or, lo there! for, behold, the kingdom of God is within you" (Luke 17:20-21).

He was speaking to the unconverted, carnal, hypocritical, lying Pharisees. Notice, "he answered *them,* and said." It was the Pharisees who asked Him the question. Were they in the CHURCH? No, never! If one thinks the Kingdom is the CHURCH—and the Kingdom was "within" the Pharisees—was THE CHURCH *within* the Pharisees? Such an assumption is rather ridiculous, now, isn't it?

Notice again, precisely WHAT JESUS SAID. Remember the CHURCH had not yet been set up. Jesus *did not say* "the Kingdom of God *shall be* set up in your hearts." He said *none* of the things people interpret *into* this verse. He said to the Pharisees "the Kingdom of God *IS*"—present tense *is,* NOW! Whatever He was saying the Kingdom of God is, He made it present tense, not future.

Luke *wrote* these words, originally, in the *Greek* language. The Greek words he wrote were translated into the English words "within you." But, if you have a Bible with the marginal references, you will notice that this is alternately rendered "*in the midst of you,*" or "*among you.*" The *context* indicates that this indeed is the better translation. If your Bible is a Moffatt translation, you will notice that the translation recognized that Jesus was talking of His *reign* or *rule,* at the head of *government.*

This is the Moffatt translation of the same verses: "[H]e answered them, 'The Reign of God is not coming as you hope to catch sight of it; no one will say, "Here it is" or "There it is," for the Reign of GOD IS NOW IN YOUR MIDST.'"

The Revised Standard Version renders it "the kingdom of God is in the midst of you." All these translations render it *present tense.*

Jesus was not talking about a church soon to be organized. He was not talking about sentiments in the mind or heart. He was talking about His REIGN, as the Messiah! The Pharisees were not asking Him about a church. They knew nothing of any New Testament Church soon to be started. They were not

asking about a pretty sentiment. They knew, from the prophecies of Daniel, Isaiah, Jeremiah and others, that their Messiah
was to come. They overlooked completely the prophecies of
His first appearing as the "Lamb of God," to be slain for the
sins of humanity—being born as a babe, growing up, being
rejected and despised by them, as recorded in Isaiah 53. They
looked only to the prophecies of His *Second* Coming as the all-
conquering and ruling KING. This the Pharisees anticipated as
the Kingdom of God.

WORLD-RULING GOVERNMENT

Jesus set them straight. He explained that it would not be a
local or limited kingdom for the Jews only. It would not be
merely one of many human and visible kingdoms which men
could point out or see, and say, "This is it, *here*"; or "that is the
Kingdom, over *there*." But He, Himself, was born to be the KING
of that Kingdom, as He plainly told Pilate (John 18:36-37). The
Bible uses the terms "king" and "kingdom" interchangeably
(see Daniel 7:17-18, 23). The KING of the future Kingdom was,
then and there, standing *in the midst of them*. And in the language in which He spoke to them, that is precisely what He
said—as the marginal rendering and other translations state.

Jesus went on, in the following verses, to describe His
Second Coming, *when* the Kingdom of God shall rule ALL THE
EARTH. In Luke 17:24 He refers to lightning flashing, just as
in Matthew 24:27, describing His Second Coming to RULE the
whole world. Luke 17:26—as it was in the days of Noah, so
shall it be when Christ comes in power and glory as world
Ruler. Verse 30—the day when He is *revealed*.

Plainly, Jesus was not saying that the Kingdom of God was
within those Christ-hating, hypocritical Pharisees. Nor was He
saying that the Church would be the Kingdom.

Now continue with the other scriptures, and it becomes
very PLAIN!

Jesus distinctly said that those Pharisees *would not be in* the
Kingdom of God. To them, He said: "There shall be weeping
and gnashing of teeth, when ye [you Pharisees] shall see
Abraham, and Isaac, and Jacob, and all the prophets, *in the
kingdom of God*, and you yourselves thrust out. And they shall

come from the east, and from the west, and from the north, and from the south, and shall sit down *in the kingdom of God*" (Luke 13:28-29).

The Kingdom of God is something men shall ENTER—at the resurrection of the just! Yet Abraham is *not there yet* (see Hebrews 11:13, 39-40).

HAS NOT YET APPEARED

But one may ask, did not Jesus Christ say the Kingdom of God was "at hand"? Yes, we quoted this, from Mark 1:15. This naturally led some to mistake what He said, and what He meant, and assume the Kingdom of God was established and set up during Jesus's ministry. Thus some supposed it was the Church.

But Jesus did not say the Kingdom of God had been established. It was now being *preached* (Luke 16:16). He did not say it was already here. Jesus, Himself, corrected this false notion. Jesus "added and spake a parable ... because they thought that the kingdom of God should immediately appear" (Luke 19:11). WHY did Jesus speak this parable? Because some, even then, mistakenly thought the Kingdom *should immediately appear*— because some thought it would be THE CHURCH!

Now continue: "He said therefore, A certain nobleman went into a far country to receive for himself a kingdom, and to return" (verse 12). Christ is that "nobleman." He is speaking of His ascension to the throne of God His Father, in heaven. Notice, He went there to be *given* rulership of the Kingdom— to receive the Kingdom. Notice, too, He is to return, when He has received it! *He has not yet returned!* Other scriptures explain this. We will turn to them a little later.

Continuing the parable, spoken *because* some thought the Kingdom of God was immediately, then, in the first century, to appear: "And it came to pass, that when he was returned, having received the kingdom, then he commanded these servants to be called unto him, to whom he had given the money, that he might know how much every man had gained by trading" (verse 15). When Christ returns, we shall all be called before the judgment seat of Christ—to give account!

Now notice in verse 17, the one who had gained 10 pounds is given authority to RULE CITIES—"have thou authority over ten cities"! To the one who had gained five pounds, he said, "Be thou also over five cities" (verse 19).

This is speaking of the SECOND COMING OF CHRIST—and of His delegating *authority to rule* to saints converted during this Christian era, between Christ's first and second appearings on Earth.

This parable, then, was spoken to make clear to us that the Kingdom of God is a literal GOVERNMENT, to be set up AT CHRIST'S SECOND COMING—*and not before!* The CHURCH, then, *cannot* be the Kingdom of God. But the true Church of God is to be *changed,* by a resurrection and instantaneous change from mortal to immortal, INTO the Kingdom of God. The Church, when all its members have been changed to immortality, shall BECOME the Kingdom of God. But it is not, now, the Kingdom!

SAINTS TO RULE

Now read the description of Christ's actual *receiving* authority to RULE the Kingdom. He is the nobleman who went to heaven to receive this kingship, and to return.

We have already seen how the Prophet Daniel recorded the setting up of the Kingdom of God—*at Christ's coming*—to consume all present national governments on Earth, and set up the world-ruling Kingdom of God. This was recorded in the second chapter. Notice now chapter seven:

"I saw in the night visions, and, behold, one like the Son of man [Christ] came with the clouds of heaven, and came to the Ancient of days, and they brought him near before him" (verse 13). Jesus continually referred to Himself as the "Son of man"—all through Matthew, Mark, Luke and John. Christ ascended to heaven in clouds (Acts 1:9). He ascended to the very throne of God in heaven (Mark 16:19). Now continue:

"And there was given him dominion, and glory, and a kingdom, that all people, nations, and languages, should serve him: his dominion is an everlasting dominion, which shall not pass away, and his kingdom that which shall not be destroyed" (Daniel 7:14).

That is plain! Christ ascended to the throne of God in heaven. God is sovereign over the entire universe. This vision shows God Almighty, Father of the resurrected living Christ, conferring on Christ dominion. Dominion means sovereign or supreme ruling authority. Also given to Him was "a kingdom." Where is that Kingdom to be? It says "a kingdom, that all people, nations, and languages, should serve him." The people, and the nations speaking different languages, are here on Earth. He is given dominion over ALL NATIONS—the whole world!

IMPORTANT WORD "UNTIL"

Now will you read, in your own Bible, Acts 3:21? It says the heavens have received Jesus Christ UNTIL—not permanently, just *until*—a certain time. Until *when?* Until the times of RESTITUTION of all things. Restitution means restoration to a former state or condition. It is speaking of restoring God's laws, God's government—of restoring happiness and universal PEACE.

In this seventh chapter of Daniel, the prophet had experienced a dream, and visions. He had seen four wild animals. Notice verse 16; *the interpretation* begins verse 17. This is GOD's inspired interpretation—not mine: "These great beasts, which are four, are four kings, which shall arise out of the earth. But the saints of the most High shall take the KINGDOM, and possess the kingdom for ever, even for ever and ever" (Daniel 7:17-18).

Notice it! Not *only* is Christ to rule—but the *saints*—that is, converted true Christians—those begotten as sons of God—are to take and possess the Kingdom! They are to rule under, and *with*, Christ! In the New Testament it is recorded that converted saints are co-heirs with Christ!

In this same seventh chapter, Daniel explained another power. The fourth beast of his dream—the fourth empire (the Roman Empire)—was pictured as an animal having 10 horns, explained here and in Revelation 13 and 17 as 10 revivals, or resurrections, of the Roman Empire, after its original fall in A.D. 476. But among them—after A.D. 476—arose another little horn—a religious kingdom, actually ruling over the last seven of the other "horns," or revived Roman kingdoms (verse 20).

Now read about this "little horn"—the religious kingdom—verse 21: "I beheld, and the same horn made war with the saints, and prevailed against them; UNTIL [*note, another "UNTIL"*] the Ancient of days came, and judgment was given to the saints of the most High; and the time came that the saints possessed the kingdom."

The saints—then no longer human flesh and blood, but immortal—are to possess the Kingdom, at the Second Coming of Christ!

Jesus Christ makes that plain. It is Christ who is speaking in Revelation 3:21, and 2:26-27: "To him that overcometh will I grant to sit with me in my throne, even as I also overcame, and am set down with my Father in his throne." The Father's throne is in heaven—where Jesus Christ is *now*; but Christ's throne, in which the saints shall sit with Him, is the throne of David, in Jerusalem (Luke 1:32).

Further: "And he that overcometh, and keepeth my works unto the end, to him will I give power over the nations: And he shall rule them with a rod of iron...."

CAN'T KNOW THE TIME

After His resurrection, on the Mount of Olives at the very hour of His ascension to heaven, Jesus was explaining to His disciples how they would receive the inspiring God-begetting POWER of the Holy Spirit on the approaching day of Pentecost.

His disciples wanted to know whether the Kingdom of God was to be set up *at that time! The* CHURCH *was* established on that imminent day of Pentecost. Was *that* CHURCH, then, to be the setting up of the Kingdom?

"Lord," they asked, "wilt thou *at this time* restore again the kingdom to Israel?" (Acts 1:6).

Jesus again made plain that the Church is *not* the Kingdom.

"And he said unto them, It is not for you to know the times or the seasons, which the Father hath put in his own power. But ye shall receive power, after that the Holy Ghost [Spirit] is come upon you: and ye shall be witnesses unto me both in Jerusalem, and in all Judaea, and in Samaria, and unto the uttermost part of the earth. And when he had spoken these things, while they beheld, he was taken up; and a cloud received him out of their sight" (verses 7-9).

The commission He had given the CHURCH was to preach His gospel to all the world. They were to receive the Holy Spirit, begetting them as saints—as Christians—putting them into

God's Church. This would infuse them with the power to carry out the mission of the Church. But it was NOT the setting up of the Kingdom of God. Of that they were not to know the time.

Just what did Jesus mean, "It is not for you to know the times or the seasons"? He explained it another time. It is recorded in Matthew 24:36: There He was speaking of the end of this world, and His Second Coming:

"But of that day and hour knoweth no man, no, not the angels of heaven, but my Father only." He was speaking of His Second Coming and the setting up of the Kingdom, the time of which no man knows, but only the Father.

However, though we do not, even now, know the day or the hour, *we do know,* from God's prophecies, *that it is today very near!* Notice this, in Luke 21:25-32: He had been foretelling the world events, *right now beginning,* leading to "distress of nations" in world troubles and world wars, "with perplexity"—"[m]en's hearts failing them for fear, and for looking after those things which are coming on the earth"— world trouble such as never before experienced. "[W]hen ye see these things come to pass, know ye that the kingdom of God is nigh at hand. Verily I say unto you, This generation shall not pass away, till all be fulfilled."

So all signs show we *are in* the very last generation of this present evil world.

THE TWO FATEFUL ALTERNATIVES

This world trouble began in 1914, with World War I. There was a recess from 1918 until 1939. We are in a second recess now. But now at last we have nuclear energy. We have hydrogen bombs stockpiled in such power and volume that they could blast all human life off this planet several times over. There are other destructive weapons today in existence, any of which could erase humanity from the Earth.

Today world-famous scientists say only a super world government can prevent world cosmocide. Yet MEN cannot and *will not* get together to form such a world-ruling government.

It's time we face the hard, cold, realistic FACT: Humanity has two alternatives: either there *is* an almighty, all-powerful GOD who is about to step in and set up THE KINGDOM OF GOD to rule all nations with supernatural and supra-national *FORCE* to bring us PEACE—or else all human life will be obliterated (Matthew 24:22).

But the recent "recess" will soon erupt into *nuclear* World War III—called, in biblical prophecy, the "Great Tribulation" (Matthew 24:21-22). But God will cut short that final supreme world trouble, and send Christ again to Earth as KING of kings, LORD of lords—to restore God's *government* by the world-ruling KINGDOM OF GOD!

）

You Can UNDERSTAND the Bible!

B ELIEVE IT OR NOT, the Bible was written for our day—this generation! No book is as up to date as the Bible. It explains the causes of present world conditions—it reveals what's ahead in the next few years. In its pages are the *solutions* to every problem we face in life—from personal and family relationships to national economics and foreign policy.

Yet, ironically, this incredible book is the least understood of all books. Most people, when they try to read it, find that they simply cannot understand it. Many assume it is irrelevant and out of date for our modern age.

But *you* can understand the Bible!

Herbert W. Armstrong College has been helping thousands to learn both the meaning of current events and the true *purpose* of life through the *Herbert W. Armstrong College Bible Correspondence Course.* Over 50,000 students from around the world have enrolled in this unique, 36-lesson course of biblical understanding.

This course has been designed to guide you through a systematic study of your own Bible—the Bible is the only textbook. Best of all—these lessons are absolutely free! There is no cost or obligation—ever.

Periodic tests, graded by Herbert W. Armstrong College staff, will help you evaluate your progress. New 16-page lessons will be sent to you after each test.

Why delay? Begin to *understand* your Bible today! Simply call, visit us online or write to the address nearest you (contact information is all on the next page) and ask to be enrolled in the *Herbert W. Armstrong College Bible Correspondence Course.*

Join over 50,000 who have already enrolled in this FREE Bible course, and begin to really understand your entire Bible for the first time!

CONTACT INFORMATION

To reach the Philadelphia Church of God to order literature or to request a visit from one of God's ministers:

Visit us online: www.pcog.org

In North America, call us toll-free: 1-800-772-8577

MAILING ADDRESSES WORLDWIDE

United States: Philadelphia Church of God, P.O. Box 3700, Edmond, OK 73083

Canada: Philadelphia Church of God, P.O. Box 315, Milton, ON L9T 4Y9

Caribbean: Philadelphia Church of God, P.O. Box 2237, Chaguanas, Trinidad, W.I.

Britain, Europe, Middle East, India and Sri Lanka: Philadelphia Church of God, P.O. Box 900, Northampton NN5 9AL, United Kingdom

Africa: Philadelphia Church of God, P.O. Box 2969, Durbanville 7551, South Africa

Australia and the Pacific Isles: Philadelphia Church of God, P.O. Box 375, Narellan N.S.W. 2567, Australia

New Zealand: Philadelphia Church of God, P.O. Box 6088, Howick Glenview, Hamilton 3246

Philippines: Philadelphia Church of God, P.O. Box 52143, Angeles City Post Office, 2009 Pampanga

Latin America: Philadelphia Church of God, Attn: Spanish Department, P.O. Box 3700, Edmond, OK 73083 United States